The
Soccer Referee's
Manual

A

ENDORSED BY
THE FOOTBALL ASSOCIATION

The Soccer Referee's Manual

David Ager

A & C Black · London

First published 1994 by
A & C Black (Publishers) Ltd
35 Bedford Row, London WC1R 4JH

ISBN 0 7136 3988 1

A CIP catalogue record for this book
is available from the British Library.

Acknowledgements
Photographs on the front cover, back cover
and pages 8, 17, 56, 68, 75, 84, 87, 88, 93, 102,
107 and 116 courtesy of Sporting Pictures
(UK) Ltd. Photographs on pages 10, 24, 52, 94
and 110 courtesy of Nigel Farrow.
Photographs on pages 2 and 118 courtesy of
Professional Sport. Photograph on page 83
courtesy of Allsport UK Ltd.
Diagrams by Taurus Graphics.

Typeset by ABM Typographics Limited, Hull
Printed and bound in Great Britain by
The Cromwell Press, Melksham, Wiltshire

Contents

Foreword

The Soccer Referee's Manual is an in-depth study of the laws of the game, and it is particularly suited to candidates on the FA referees course, with its emphasis not only on the laws, but also on their practical application.

The role of the referee has become more onerous in the past few years, and in evaluating his duties, tasks and responsibilities, this book will also provide interest to all who enjoy this great game, including players, managers, coaches and the media. The manual contains many illustrated examples, along with test questions aimed at assisting the trainee referee, and testing the knowledge of more experienced officials.

David Ager is a most respected Cornwall County FA referee and FA Licensed Referee Instructor. This, his first book, will prove an excellent resource for referees at all levels of the game, and for anyone interested in soccer.

Martin Bodenham
National List referee
FIFA referee

Introduction

Soccer was developed in the nineteenth century as a game for public schoolboys in an attempt to develop character, instil teamwork and provide an outlet for youthful high spirits. From these roots it has become one of the world's leading sports, played by millions of people. From being a sport purely for young men, soccer is now being played increasingly by women and older men.

Although the game is primarily about participating, it is impossible for competitive soccer to be played without referees. As society has become more and more competitive, so soccer has become more concerned with winning. This has not only led to the referee becoming a more important figure in the game, but it has also placed referees under much greater pressure.

The main aim of this book is to prepare candidates for the FA Class 3 Referee's Certificate. This is the starting point for a career in refereeing. By working through the manual, the reader can gain an understanding of the laws of the game, and their application in practice.

A second aim is to help the practising referee to refine and develop his game, and to revise his knowledge and understanding of the laws. The material will encourage referees to give some thought as to how they approach the game, and the techniques used to apply the laws.

The third aim is to provide players, spectators, enthusiasts and the media with an opportunity to gain an understanding of the laws of soccer, and the job of the referee. As the decisions of referees become increasingly important, and the subject of continuing controversy and argument, an awareness of the refereeing role becomes more valuable to anyone with a love of the game.

For the sake of brevity and clarity, the manual is written using the male gender throughout. The author wishes to make it clear that this is in no way intended as a slight against women's involvement in soccer generally, or in refereeing in particular. Just as increasing numbers of women are now playing the game, so more women are taking up refereeing, a trend that is greatly welcomed.

Note Other than those given in the Cooper Test of physical fitness, all measurements are in imperial units.

Unit 1
The referee and linesmen

Part 1
Law 5 – The referee

At first it may seem strange that the law relating to referees is tucked away in fifth place. However, it is not so strange when we consider that in the early years of soccer there was no mention of referees in the laws of the game at all. The reason for this was simple – there were no referees! Any dispute was dealt with by a discussion between the two captains, and for most decisions the players were assumed to be honest and sporting so that no disagreement would occur over which team was entitled to a throw-in, or whether a goal kick or corner should be awarded. Very quickly, as soccer became more popular and more competitive, disagreements became more common, so that the need for some sort of arbitration arose.

The first referees were umpires who sat outside the field of play and only gave decisions when requested to do so by the captains in situations where they had failed to come to an agreement. Soon, the referee was expected to impose decisions on the two teams, and thus he entered the field of play to ensure a closer view.

The evolution of the role of the referee from that of an 'arbitrator' or 'adjudicator' to that of 'controller', expected to make all the decisions within the game, necessitated a clear definition of his powers. These are found in Law 5, with the following law devoted to the linesmen.

Law 5 is broken down into ten parts, each defining either a duty which the referee must perform, or a power which he may use where necessary in the game.

(A) Enforce the laws

The referee has a duty to enforce the laws. Quite simply, that is the prime reason for him being there. The referee is expected to uphold and interpret the laws of the game in order to ensure that a fair, sensible and competitive game of soccer takes place.

Left Soccer is a game. It is meant to be enjoyed. Referees should keep a sense of humour and aim to enjoy the game and help others to enjoy it too

(B) Refraining from penalising in cases where he would be giving an advantage to the offending team

It is often the case that although an infringement has occurred, the award of a free kick would be to the advantage of the offending team. A simple example is that of a player who breaks through the defence and although fouled by an opponent, retains his footing to have a good chance on goal. A free kick in this situation would allow the defence to re-group, and thus gain a considerable advantage. Frequently, the referee has to sum up very quickly in his own mind whether or not a free kick should be given. The referee cannot change his mind and give the free kick. If, therefore, the advantage does not come about, the referee has little option but to allow play to continue.

Perhaps the best advice to a new referee is don't worry too much about the advantage clause until you are more confident about its use. It's better to give a few too many unnecessary free kicks than to see the game go out of control because you are trying too hard to play the advantage. Also, there are some circumstances in which applying the advantage clause may *not* be advisable. For example, if a really serious foul or an assault has taken place, the game should normally be stopped immediately, so that the player(s) concerned can be dealt with. Although it is possible to caution or send off a player when the game stops later on, failure to do so quickly may result in an ugly situation turning into an impossible one, with players taking the law into their own hands and a brawl developing.

Another situation where the advantage clause should be treated with respect is if the offence has occurred in or near the penalty area of the non-offending team. It is very tempting, and often very sensible, to allow play to continue without a free kick where, following an offside or a foul on a defender, the goalkeeper has the ball in his hands and can clear it quickly upfield. The referee should, however, treat this with some caution if there is any risk of the goalkeeper, or another defender, not getting to the ball, in which case the advantage gained by the attacking side will be consider-able. Another danger is if the goalkeeper has been unfairly challenged but retains the ball. He may prefer to take a few seconds to recover before playing on, and a free kick would be welcome here. If there is a danger of further confrontation between the players following the original challenge, then this also should be taken into account and a free kick awarded.

Finally, it is very important for the referee to remember to clearly in-form the players that he is applying the advantage clause. He should extend both arms forwards, and shout 'Play on! – Advantage!', so that the players know that he has acknowledged an infringement. Failure to do this will mean they assume that he has missed the offence, and they will begin to lose confidence in him.

(C) Keep a record of the game; act as a timekeeper...

It is important that the referee keeps a clear record of the game. To do this, referees have a match record card, an example of which is illustrated below.

COMPETITION					DATE:	
TEAMS	H		A		CAPTAIN'S Nos.	
					H	A
COLOURS		K.O.		K.O.		
GOALS	1st		SCORE		SCORE	
	2nd					
	NAME/No.	CODE	NAME/No.	CODE		
CAUTIONS AND DISMISSALS						
SUBSTITUTES					LINESMEN	
					H	
					A	

Fig. 1 Example of a clean match record card

Perhaps the most important feature of the card is the score. It is strange how easy it is for the referee to lose count of the score in the game, and a careful record will ensure that this error is not made. With the card, there is a space for writing in the half-time scores so that if an entry is made in the wrong place in the second half, it can be discovered more easily. I write the half-time score down in words rather than numbers in order to make errors less likely. The importance of this cannot be underestimated and I can illustrate this from an experience of a friend of mine.

He was playing in a cup quarter-final with the score standing at 2-1 to his team. With 10 minutes left, his side scored a third goal and, at the end of 90 minutes, the score stood at 3-1. As the teams left the field, the referee called them back, explaining that extra time had to be played since the score was 2-2! Both teams insisted that the score was 3-1 but the referee was adamant. The game went into extra time and the side that had really lost 3-1 scored a goal, making the score 2-3 to them, according to the referee. The side that felt it had won the game in 90 minutes appealed, taking the secretary and captain of the other side along as witnesses on its behalf. The referee, however, stuck to his story and, since he is the sole judge of what happened in the game, this was accepted by the appeals committee. I suspect that this story is rather unusual, but it does illustrate the great importance of maintaining a clear record of the game.

It is also important to write down clearly the time of kick-off. A good tip here is to also indicate the time the game is due to end. This gives an extra check on when the referee will need to blow for the end of the half, and saves some mental arithmetic during the match, when he will have more important things to think about.

Normally, the FA will require the *full* name of the culprit if anyone has been cautioned or dismissed, so the referee should make sure that he has this information. It is also useful to put the time of the offence down. This helps the referee to distinguish between incidents in a game, and is also

COMPETITION	MIDLAND AMATEUR LEAGUE						DATE: 31/11/93
TEAMS	H ROSE AND CROWN FC			A HARRISONS BREWERY FC			CAPTAIN'S Nos. H 6 A 5
COLOURS	RED		K.O. 2·30 −3·15	BLUE		K.O. 3·20 −4·05	CAUTION & DISMISSAL CODES
GOALS 1st	| |		SCORE 2			SCORE 2	D Dissent UC Ungentlemanly Conduct
GOALS 2nd	|	|		| |		3	P Persistantly infringing the laws of the game
	NAME/No.		CODE	NAME/No.		CODE	E Entering or re-entering the field of play without permission
CAUTIONS AND DISMISSALS	Alan KEAST 2·45		U.C.	Sid THOMAS 3·05		V	
	Ray BROWN 3·30		D				V Violent Conduct
							SF Serious Foul Play
							F Foul or Abusive language
							SE Second cautionable offence
SUBSTITUTES	John POPE	✓		Peter GEORGE			
	Peter WALTERS			Kevin ADAMS	✓		
	Bruce TAYLOR	✓		Peter THORPE			LINESMEN
	Simon HARRIS			Tony REYNOLDS			H John SWAN
	Paul BARKER			Keith ROWE			A John ROBERTS

Fig. 2 Example of a completed match record card

required by the FA in the report. On the previous page there is a completed match record card, which illustrates the points made.

(D) Have discretionary power to stop the game for any infringement of the laws, and to suspend or terminate the game wherever . . . he deems such stoppage necessary

Here the referee is empowered to stop the game for free kicks, etc. as required, a power which is, perhaps, fairly obvious. If spectators go out of control, or the light fades, or the weather makes the game impossible to complete in safety, then the referee should abandon it. If he does this, it is important to report the matter to the appropriate authority (either the league concerned or the FA, depending under whose auspices the game is being played). They, and they alone, have the power to determine whether the game should be replayed or whether the score at the time of abandonment should stand. An important point to remember is that once the referee has decided to abandon the game, he should *not* allow himself to be talked into changing his mind. This can create enormous problems for himself. If, for example, a hailstorm descends, he can temporarily stop the game and delay a decision as to whether to continue, but should not be talked into returning once he has made up his mind and has communicated his decision to the two teams.

(E) From the time he enters the field of play, caution any player guilty of misconduct . . .

I will deal with cautions more fully in a later unit, but for now it is worth remembering that the referee has the power to caution players where appropriate *from the moment he enters* the field of play. This means that he can quite legitimately caution a player *before* the game has actually started. The entry to the field of play is not very clearly defined, but it is fair to say that the referee's powers here begin pretty well from the point when he leaves the dressing room.

(F) Allow no person other than the players and linesmen to enter the field without his permission

Here the referee is given the power to stop anyone else from entering the field of play. This is very important. If a player is injured, then it may be necessary for the trainer to come on the field to attend to him. It is not necessary for an entourage of trainer, manager, substitute and a couple of supporters to come on as well. If there is some controversy in the incident which led to the player being injured, then the arrival of these unwanted people may result in a confrontation which he may find hard to control. As with so much in refereeing, prevention is better than cure, so the referee should be firm and *only* allow those who *have* to be on the field, to enter it.

It is now possible for coaching from the side lines to occur, provided the coaching takes place in the 'technical area'. This means the area immediately around the team bench. Referees should beware of allowing coaching to be undertaken elsewhere, as it may distract opponents unfairly.

(G) Stop the game . . . if a player has been seriously injured . . .

The referee should stop the game if a player appears to be badly hurt. If a player is only slightly injured, then he can be dealt with *off* the field of play. Making a judgment here can be difficult for the referee. The best advice is, if in doubt, stop the game and don't move the player. This is especially important if the player has sustained a head injury. Although television has, in recent years, highlighted the play-acting of players in the professional game, this is very rare in junior soccer. When a player goes down injured, it is usually best to give him the benefit of the doubt and delay the game. The referee should not be talked into trying to move the player if he judges it unwise. The players will be looking to the referee to take sensible decisions, so he should err on the side of caution and take no sides. If possible referees should try to take some first aid training.

A few years ago, I refereed an evening game in which the home goalkeeper seriously injured his knee in a collision. We kept him warm and comfortable, and, despite the gathering gloom, delayed the re-start of the game until an ambulance had arrived. When it did, the medics took 15 minutes to put the player into the ambulance, vindicating my decision not to attempt to inexpertly move him off the field, despite pressure from several players who wanted him moved to the touch-line so that the game could continue.

(H) Send off . . . any player who . . . is guilty of violent conduct, etc.

Later in the manual I will look in more detail at the business of sending off players for serious misconduct. This clause simply establishes the power of the referee to take his action. A point worth remembering is that any referee who is in charge of a game played between FA registered teams has this power. If, therefore, the club secretary takes over in the absence of an official referee, he too can caution or send off players.

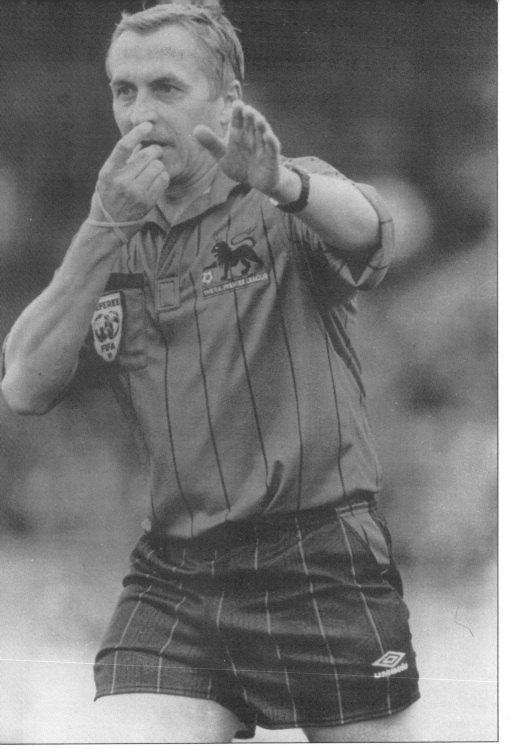

It is essential for the referee to keep alert at all times during the game

(I) Signal for the re-commencement of the game after all stoppages

To make it clear that you wish the game to re-start, it is necessary to signal this to the players. This does not necessarily mean blowing the whistle; you could simply shout to the players to continue. For many stoppages, it is best to encourage the game to continue to flow, so for throw-ins and goal kicks, or minor infringements, there is little need for any signal. If, however, the game has been stopped for a reasonable period of time, then it is best to use the whistle to make it clear that you are re-starting after a break. I will look at aspects of this later in the course, when we consider free kicks and other re-starts.

(J) Decide that the ball conforms to Law 2

The final clause in Law 5 relates to the match ball. This is considered in more detail in another unit, but for now it is worth remembering that you are responsible for ensuring that the ball provided by the club is acceptable. A well organised club will provide this before the start of the game – if you are unlucky, it is presented to you, covered in mud, at the centre spot as you are about to spin the coin, and it is often at the wrong pressure. The referee should try, if at all possible, to get hold of the ball well before the start of the game.

Some other points are worth noting. The first is that it is important to realise that the referee, once having re-started the game, cannot reverse his decision. If the game has not re-started he *can* do so, for example in the light of a linesman's advice. An example of this is when a goal has been scored, but the referee cancels his decision to give offside following consultation with a linesman.

Another point to remember is that referees should be distinctive in dress from the players. This is normally no great problem since, you would think, no team is likely to arrive dressed in black. In fact, about the third game I refereed involved a college team that arrived on the field wearing black shirts. I walked over to an adjacent field to seek advice from a more experienced referee: 'That's all right', he said rather cynically, 'just collect your fee and go home. You can't referee them.' I wandered over to the team to tell them that I couldn't referee an all-black team. 'That's OK', said the captain, 'they're reversible.' Sure enough, the players took off the shirts and turned them inside out to reveal a pale blue colour. It is worth remembering, of course, that occasionally teams do play in dark blue when the referee agrees to wear a different colour.

The law states that to win the respect of players and spectators, the referee should:

(1) learn and understand every law
(2) be absolutely fair and impartial in every decision
(3) keep physically fit and in good training.

Although this book should give you a good understanding of the laws of the game, referees must make every effort to keep up-to-date, and they must refresh their knowledge. This can be done by joining the local branch of the Referees' Association, where refereeing problems and the application of the laws are discussed. Failure to understand the laws of the game leads to the charge of inconsistency and reduces the standing of referees, and it will also impede the progress of the individual.

Being absolutely fair and impartial may appear to be obvious, but can, at times, be a little difficult to achieve. Where the referee has had more pressure put on him from one team, it may be that he begins to weaken, and gives that team more '50-50' decisions than he should. Some teams will try to 'soften up' the referee by continually questioning or commenting on his decisions, and the referee should be aware of this before he loses his impartiality.

Another problem may occur if a referee feels that a decision in the early part of the game to give a penalty, for example, was unfair, and he then tries to make up for this later in the match. This is disastrous, wins him no friends and will ensure that he loses control of the game. If he has made a bad decision, it is something he will just have to live with. If it's any consolation, referees at all levels experience this problem from time to time.

I am always amazed at the poor physical condition of a minority of referees. A lack of mobility is by no means uncommon in local parks as the red-faced, perspiring official attempts desperately to keep up with play. If the referee is reaching an advanced age, this may be understandable, but when he is in his twenties or thirties it is less forgivable. Regular physical training, consisting of road running or cardio-vascular circuits, weight training and participation in sports such as squash and badminton, are important to good refereeing. Squash is especially valuable with its emphasis on swift physical and mental responses. If you are physically fit, you are more likely to be mentally alert and this is essential to successful refereeing. English FA National List officials (those who referee at the highest level) must complete the 'Cooper Test' satisfactorily, and this is reprinted at the end of this unit.

Now – before continuing – answer the following questions, without flicking through to check the text!

Questions

(Check your answers in the text.)

Question A   When do the powers of the referee commence?

Question B   Under what circumstances should the referee stop the game?

Question C   What can the referee *not* do when he has applied the advantage clause?

Question D   For what reasons should the referee send off a player?

Question E   Can the referee reverse his decision?

Question F   What should the referee do in order to win the respect of players and spectators?

Question G   Under what circumstances should the referee allow those other than players and linesmen on to the pitch?

Question H   What can happen to a referee who fails to report misconduct which came to his notice?

Question I   Must the referee blow his whistle to signal the re-start of play?

Finally, a quick way of remembering what we have just covered is by studying this list of duties and powers.

D   Decide on disputed points. On points of fact the referee's decision is final. Decide that the ball meets with the requirements of Law 2.

U   Unauthorised persons not allowed to enter the field of play. Coaching by trainers or club officials along the boundary lines is forbidden.

T   Timekeeper. Sole judge of time. He will allow the full or agreed time, adding thereto all time lost through accident or other cause and to permit the taking of a penalty kick.

I   Injury. Stop the game and have players removed if seriously injured. If injury is slight the game shall not be stopped until ball is out of play. Players able to do so should go to the boundary line for treatment.

E   Enforce the laws.

S   Signal for re-commencement after stoppages.

P Power to penalise when ball is in or out of play, or when play is temporarily stopped. Power to refrain from penalising (advantage clause).

O Order off without previous caution a player guilty of violent conduct or using foul or abusive language.

W Warn (i.e. caution) players guilty of misconduct/ungentlemanly conduct, and if a player persists, to suspend him from the game.

E End or suspend the game whenever, by reason of the elements, interference by spectators, or other cause, he deems such stoppage necessary.

R Report to the appropriate authority as laid down in rules of competition.

S Stop the game for infringement of the laws.

The referee's equipment

It is essential that the referee arrives at the ground in good time, properly equipped. Failure to bring an essential piece of equipment, such as boots, or tunic, will present him with huge problems which, at best, will put him at a considerable disadvantage from the start, and at worst may stop him from refereeing the game altogether. Furthermore, he should ensure that his equipment is well cared for and appropriate to the task in hand.

Tunic, shorts and socks

The referee should make sure that these are clean and, if necessary, pressed. Socks, especially those with all white tops, tend to turn grey after a while. They should be replaced as soon as this happens – they are, after all, quite inexpensive to buy. It is not acceptable for a referee to turn up in dirty, mud-stained shirt and shorts.

Flags

I never cease to be amazed at the way some referees unthinkingly hand a dirty, dishevelled flag to their linesmen at the start of the game. How can a referee command respect from a club linesman if he offers him a mud-encrusted flag? It is very easy for the referee to wash his flags after a game and, if necessary, iron them before use.

Footwear

Needless to say, my earlier comments on clothing also apply to boots. These should be clean and polished. If white laces are worn, these should also be clean.

Whistle

The referee should ideally have two whistles, one spare in case of problems. It is a good idea to have them on a lanyard – just a simple length of crêpe bandage is fine – so that the whistle is easy to hand. A word of warning here – don't run with the whistle in your mouth. If the ball is unexpectedly kicked at your face, you may suffer quite serious injury to the teeth.

Spare handkerchief

The referee will need a handkerchief for his own use, but a spare one could be invaluable too. This must be clean and unused, and is needed in case a player suffers from a cut or nosebleed and needs something to stem the flow or to protect the wound until more thorough first aid is available.

Watches

The referee should have two watches – one, at least, should be a stopwatch. Several good quartz wrist-watches are now available which have this facility, and a few have been designed purely for soccer timing. Beware of some electronic stopwatches. Highly sensitive switches mean that these are often accidentally changed in the referee's pocket or hanging round his neck, and are thus of little use in a match.

Red and yellow cards

In recent times, the use of red and yellow cards has become necessary at all levels of the game. These are usually made of plastic, and come in different shapes – one oval and the other rectangular. This avoids the embarrassment caused by the referee pulling out the wrong card by mistake.

A number of other items may be taken to a match. Of course, it is important to take a **coin,** and even more important to remember to take it out on the field on play! Often, referees take an **adaptor** and a **pump.** Many less well organised junior sides may lack these basic essentials; having them available may retrieve an otherwise impossible situation. Never underestimate the ability of clubs to be disorganised and badly equipped! This leads me to another item worth taking – toilet paper. A few years ago I ran the line in a local cup final. The dressing rooms were full of players, club officials, match and league officials. A visit to the toilets, however, revealed a complete lack of paper!

Questions

(Answers on page 35.)

Question 1   What action could the referee take if he found that a linesman was unreliable and inefficient, or biased?

Question 2   During a match, a team disagrees with the referee's decision and walks off in protest. After several minutes, the players cool down and express a wish to re-start the game. Should the referee now re-start?

Question 3   The referee is struck by the ball, which temporarily stuns him. The ball rebounds and enters the goal. Should the goal be allowed to stand, even though he couldn't see it?

Question 4   Just as the referee is about to start a game, he notices a player who is under suspension. Should he refuse to allow him to play?

Part 2

Law 6 – Linesmen

According to Law 6, linesmen are required to do the following.

(1) Indicate when the ball has gone out of play for a corner, goal kick or throw-in.
(2) Indicate which side is entitled to the throw-in.
(3) Indicate when a substitute is required.

If the linesman is neutral, he can also be asked to indicate foul play and misconduct where the incident has taken place on the referee's blind side.

Although not specifically mentioned in the *Referee's Chart,* linesmen – especially when neutral – are normally expected to indicate offside.

Many referees argue that running the line is a much more difficult job than refereeing. In addition to looking for the ball going out of play, a linesman must be aware of the probability of a player being offside when the ball is kicked forwards. In flagging for a foul, a linesman may have to take into account the manner in which the referee is handling the game. Is he likely to prefer to play advantage, for example? Another problem is that a linesman is far nearer than the referee to any abuse or 'constructive criticism' on offer from supporters. Finally, while being cautious of abusing the referee, often players seem to regard the linesmen as easier game for comments and argument.

So, running the line well is far from easy. For a match to be well controlled, the referee and his two linesmen need to work in close co-operation. Let us start, however, by looking at the signals which the linesmen give to the referee. Firstly, there is the signal for a throw-in. The linesman points the flag clearly in the direction of play of the side which is entitled to the throw.

Fig. 3 Throw-in (to the side playing from right to left as the reader looks)

Note that in the diagram below left the linesman has put the flag in his left hand. This is important because if he holds the flag in his right hand he will cover part of his face and obscure his view of the game. There is also a danger that the signal will be less clear and even ambiguous.

The linesman should also give an indication for goal kicks. This can be seen in the diagram below right, in which the linesman points clearly across the field to the goal area.

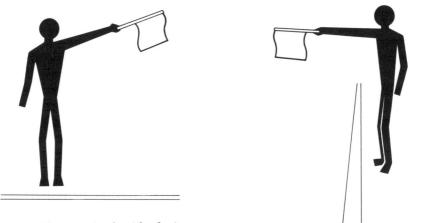

Fig. 4 Throw-in (to the side playing from left to right as the reader looks)   *Fig. 5 Goal kick*

The final signal for the ball going out of play is the award of a corner kick. Here the linesman should point his flag to the nearer corner as shown in the diagram below.

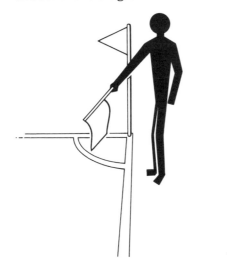

Fig. 6 Corner kick

Note that the linesman should *never* point to the far corner. This can be very confusing, with the referee unable to tell whether the signal being given by the linesman is for a goal kick, offside or a corner kick.

The signals for offside are quite simple. The linesman raises the flag with a flourish and, when seen by the referee, shows it as follows.

In the first diagram, the linesman is indicating that offside has occurred on the far side of the field of play. In the second, the offside is roughly central. In the third diagram, the offside has occurred on the linesman's side of the field. We will consider this in more detail when we study the offside law.

Fig. 7 Offside on the far side

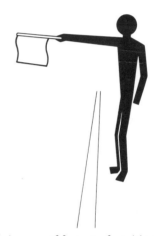

Fig. 8 Offside in a roughly central position

Fig. 9 Offside on the linesman's side of the field

There is one more signal mentioned in the laws. This is the signal for a substitution. Here the referee simply raises his flag as shown below, indicating that a team wishes to make a substitution.

Fig. 10 Substitution

Note that this signal should never be given while the ball is in play, only when the game has stopped for some reason.

Two other signals used by linesmen are not mentioned in the laws. The first of these is where the linesman puts the flag across his chest as shown below left, indicating that he is advising the referee that he should award a penalty kick.

Finally, the linesman may be asked to draw his arm horizontally across his chest to indicate that on his watch the 45 minutes of the half are completed (below right).

Fig. 11 Advising the award of a penalty kick

Fig. 12 Indicating that on his watch the 45 minutes of the half are completed

Questions

(Answers on page 35.)

Question 5   What colour should linesmen's flags be?

Question 6   Who, according to the laws, should provide the flags?

Question 7   An attack takes place in which the ball is kicked into the goal, but the referee then sees the linesman's flag raised. He goes over to the linesman who tells him that a player was in an offside position, interfering with play, and that the goal should not be awarded. What should the referee do?

Question 8   A neutral linesman sees a player assault an opponent, and draws the referee's attention to this. Unfortunately the referee has not seen the incident. What should the referee do?

The diagonal system of control

Until the 1930s, linesmen simply ran the length of the field, while the referee ran in an oval path around the field. In 1934, Sir Stanley Rous introduced the diagonal system of control in the FA Cup Final between Manchester City and Portsmouth, which he refereed. This is shown below.

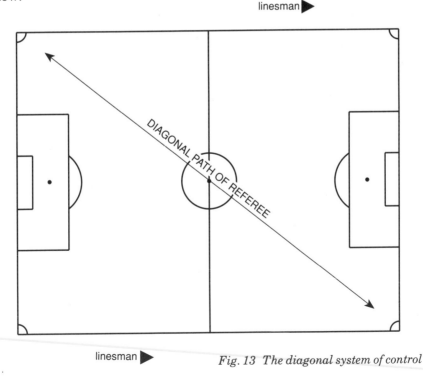

Fig. 13 The diagonal system of control

The aim of this system is to achieve the greatest possible co-operation between the referee and his linesmen, and the most efficient use of the three officials. If play is in one half of the field, the referee and one of the linesmen will be able to cover it. Note that when this happens, the referee – if he is in a good position – will be able to see not only the action of the game, but also the signals of the linesmen (for example, for offside or the ball going out of play, or for an offence committed in a position where the referee cannot see it clearly himself). The other linesman, meanwhile, has a good view of the other half, so that he can follow a quick breakaway if the ball is cleared upfield. The referee can choose to run either diagonal, incidentally. His choice will be determined by factors such as wind, sun, slope of the field, or other factors.

Linesmen

For the system to work well, there has to be a clear understanding between the referee and his linesmen before the start of the game. Normally, the linesmen will report to the referee before the start of the game to receive instructions from him as to how he intends to run the game.

Of course, there is a distinction between club linesmen and neutral linesmen. In local, junior level soccer, and even sometimes in semi-professional matches, the referee must rely entirely on club linesmen. Only in important games, such as cup finals, will the referee have neutral linesmen at this level.

Club linesmen are frequently officials of the team, often the manager or secretary, or sometimes one of the substitutes. Needless to say, quality varies considerably. The best club linesmen often take their job very seriously, and are dedicated and honest. Sometimes leagues offer a trophy to the best linesman of the season, based on marks given by the referee, and the standard can be very high. All too frequently, however, the linesman has been forced into doing a job he would far rather avoid. The result is that his commitment to the task is lacking. I have often found the linesman talking to his friends or lighting a pipe rather than involving himself in the task in hand.

Neutral linesmen are simply referees who have been appointed to run the line. As such, they have wider responsibilities than club linesmen, and the referee can come to depend on them for more support and advice than he would a club linesman. Anyone coming afresh into refereeing is unlikely to have the luxury of neutral linesmen for quite some time, but they are likely to find themselves acting as neutral linesmen fairly soon.

Briefing the linesmen

(A) Club linesmen

Before the game, the referee should explain what he wants from his linesmen. If he judges that a linesman has little interest, or is very inexperienced, this conversation can be trimmed down a little. I believe that a linesman who only gives signals for the ball out of play, for example, is better than nothing. If this is all he is able, or willing, to offer, I will accept it.

Instructions to club linesmen should include the following.

(1) The diagonal which the referee is going to run, thus determining the position of the linesmen.

(2) The forwards which the linesmen are going to 'adopt'. In other words, whether the linesmen are going to judge offside against their own or the opposition forwards. (Often referees have a local convention about which to do.)

(3) To indicate when the ball has gone out of play and to indicate which team is entitled to the throw-in, or whether to award a corner or goal kick.

(4) Check that the ball is correctly placed in the goal area for the taking of a goal kick.

(5) Stand near to the corner post and indicate if the ball goes out of play at the taking of a corner kick.

(6) Signal to indicate if a player is in an offside position when the ball is played.

The linesmen should also be told that the referee must take the final decision. A good referee, however, will always acknowledge a linesman's signal, even though he may wish to ignore or overrule it.

(B) Neutral linesmen

Here, the situation is more complicated. The referee can rely far more on neutral linesmen than he can on club linesmen, but his instructions to them need to be more wide-ranging and precise.

Instructions to neutral linesmen should thus include the following.

(1) The time. The referee and linesmen should establish the time so that all their watches are synchronised.

(2) Timing the game. Referees often ask the linesmen to give signals to indicate that there are just a few minutes left, or that the normal period of time is completed. Often, the referee will ask the senior linesman to stop his watch for injuries, or other stoppages (in line with the referee), while the junior linesman will be told to simply let his watch run through the full 45 minutes.

(3) The side of the field which each linesman will take in each half, and the diagonal which the referee will be adopting.

Normally, the senior linesman will be put on the side on which the dug-outs are placed, so that he can handle substitutions during the game.

(4) The linesmen's duties prior to the start of the game. Usually, the referee will ask the linesmen to inspect the goals before the start of the game to make sure that the nets are secure and that everything is safe and in good order.

(5) Who is the senior linesman. The senior linesman will have to take over if the referee is injured, and he thus must take note, not only of goals scored, kick-off times, etc., but also any cautions or dismissals which have been dealt with by the referee.

(6) Position to be taken at re-starts. The referee will usually tell the linesmen where he wishes them to stand at the taking of corners, penalty kicks or goal kicks.

(7) Signals. The referee may ask for certain signals from linesmen to indicate, for example, that the ball is in the correct position for a goal kick or corner kick.

(8) Throw-ins. The referee will tell the linesmen whether he wishes them to look for infringements with the feet or the hands at a throw-in.

(9) Offside. The referee will explain what he requires of the linesmen here. Often he will say 'The offsides are yours at all times', meaning that the linesmen should always keep in position to judge offside.

Occasionally the referee will ask linesmen to stand on the goal line at the taking of a free kick awarded to the attacking side near to the opposition goal. This is so that he can judge the ball going over the line, or infringements in the goal area. In this case, the referee will judge offside when the kick is taken.

(10) Misconduct. The referee will ask the linesmen to keep an eye on the game for any infringements by players. Normally this is only in the quarter (or sometimes half) of the field nearest to them. In particular, if an incident occurs off the ball which the referee does not see but the linesman does, then the linesman must inform the referee as soon as possible. If, as a result, the referee cautions or sends off a player, then the linesman who saw the incident must submit a misconduct report.

Positioning at re-starts

Much discussion is given up at Referees' Association meetings concerning the best position to take up at re-starts in the game. A good referee should be flexible about his positioning, since different games may require slightly different positions to be adopted. The following are straightforward suggestions which will illustrate some of the factors which the referee needs to consider.

Goal kicks

Here the referee takes up a position of 90° to the 'dropping zone', i.e. where he expects the ball to arrive. This is so that he can see fouls either by defenders pushing or attackers 'backing in' to opponents. It is important to remember that the dropping zone will vary from game to game according to wind strength, the overall length of the field, and the ability of players to kick the ball. The linesmen should be in position to judge offside, but it is important to remember that players cannot be offside *direct* from a goal kick.

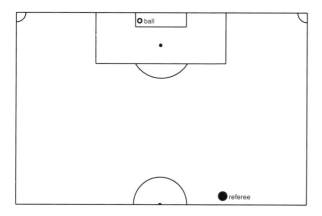

Fig. 14 Position of referee at goal kicks

Corner kicks

(A) On the referee's diagonal

On the next page the referee has placed himself in a position midway between the outer corner of the penalty area and the outer corner of the goal area. In this position he has a good view of the penalty area and in particular of the area in front of goal where incidents are most likely to occur. If the ball comes over the goal area, he can quickly move forwards to get a better view, while if the ball is cleared quickly upfield, he can make ground to cover a breakaway attack. Note that the linesman is standing a few yards from the corner post, along the goal line. He will be looking to see if the ball goes out of play. If he is a neutral linesman, he will be looking for any infringements as the ball is kicked.

(B) Off the referee's diagonal

Here the referee takes up a similar position. However, the linesman stands behind the corner post. This makes it easier for him to judge whether the ball has gone out of play from an outswinging corner which has then come back into play.

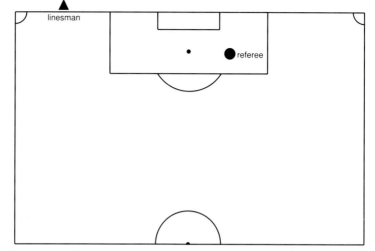

Fig. 15 Position of officials at corner kicks: on the referee's diagonal

Penalty kicks

Here the referee stands in a position where he can best judge 'encroach-ment' by players. This is where a player enters the penalty area or comes within 10 yards of the ball before it is kicked. He can also see any miscon-duct by the kicker, and ensure that the player nominated to take the kick actually takes it. The linesman judges whether a goal is scored or not, and also whether the goalkeeper moves his feet before the kick is taken.

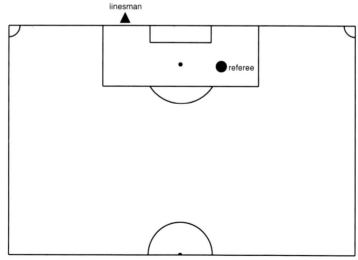

Fig. 16 Position of officials at penalty kicks

Answers

Question 1   He is quite entitled to dispense with the linesman's services if he is dissatisfied with him. He should beware, however, because in a junior game he may find that he is the only linesman available. In this situation he may only wish to get rid of him in the last resort.

Question 2   This is a situation in which he needs to use his common sense. If the team has walked off for several minutes, he would be wise to abandon the game. If he has already stated or threatened that he will end the game unless the team returns immediately, he would be foolish to continue. He should remember to send a report regarding the incident to the appropriate authority.

Question 3   Unless he has a neutral linesman who has seen the incident clearly, he should not award a goal which he has not clearly seen. He must re-start play with a dropped ball when he has recovered. If he has been knocked out for more than a very brief time, he would be well advised not to continue the game, and if necessary to seek medical advice.

Question 4   He cannot really refuse him permission to play. The referee is there to referee a soccer match, not to decide on the eligibility of players to play. It would be sensible, however, to warn the club secretary concerned, and also check to see if the player's name has been correctly entered on the team sheet which the referee signs at the end of the game. If it has, the appropriate authority will doubtlessly pick this up and take action.

Question 5   The laws require that flags have *bright vivid colours.*

Question 6   According to the laws, the home club should provide the flags. The referee should not depend on this, however, as very few clubs actually provide them and, when they do, they are often virtually unusable.

Question 7   Provided the referee has not re-started the game, he can change his decision. If he is happy with the advice of the linesman, he may give an indirect free kick for offside. The referee, however, *always* has the final word and is ultimately responsible.

Question 8   In this case, the referee should send the offending player off for violent conduct. Because he himself has not seen the incident, the referee cannot submit a detailed misconduct report, but must rely on the neutral linesman to do this.

The Cooper Test of physical fitness

(1) Repetition speed test

Referees are required to sprint a distance of 25 metres within 5 seconds, and to repeat this **eight** times with a 25-second rest between each run. The referee returns to the starting line during the 25-second rest period after each 25-metre run. Total test time = (5 seconds + 25 seconds) × 8 = 240 seconds (4 minutes).

A 15-minute recovery/rest period is allowed before the second test.

(2) Endurance test

The number of metres run on level ground in 12 minutes will be recorded, but anything less than 2600 metres will be considered a failure. Candidates must run for the full 12 minutes, and *not* stop when reaching the minimum distance, which applies irrespective of age.

Other minimum levels of performance which you *should* be able to achieve are: 400-metre run, 75 seconds; 50-metre run, 8 seconds; shuttle run 4 × 10 metres, 11.5 seconds.

The following table will give you some idea of your performance in relation to your fitness. (All values are the number of metres run over level ground for the duration of 12 minutes.)

Age	18–29	30–39	40–49	50–59
Very poor	−1750	−1500	−1250	−1000
Poor	1760–2240	1510–1990	1250–1740	1010–1490
In condition	2250–2750	2000–2550	1750–2250	1500–2000
Excellent	2760–	2510–	2260–	2010–

Unit 2
Laws 1-3

Part 1
Law 1 – The field of play

Law 1 is concerned with the field of play. Originally, before the laws of the game were properly set out in the middle of the nineteenth century, soccer was played on an area which might vary greatly according to the local geography. The need to standardise the laws so that different teams could play with some certainty as to what to expect, led to a set of rules which determined the overall size and shape of the playing area, along with the internal areas such as the goal and penalty areas, and the goals themselves. These are all contained in this law.

The external dimensions of a soccer field allow for some leeway, so that they can be adjusted to local conditions. In an international game, the dimensions are much more restricted to ensure a greater conformity.

Questions
(Answers on page 49.)

Question 1　What is the maximum and minimum length of a soccer field?

Question 2　What is the maximum and minimum width of a soccer field?

Question 3　What shape should the field of play *always* be?

As you can see, the field can vary greatly in its overall dimensions. Clubs can legitimately use this to their own advantage. Some years ago, Bolton Wanderers deliberately narrowed their playing area by 10 yards or so when playing at home to Preston North End. In those days, Tom Finney was playing on the wing for Preston, and he liked to play as wide as possible. The narrow field cramped his style and gave Bolton an advantage which was within the laws.

In most situations, it is unlikely that a club will have marked out a playing area which is too big, although I have known clubs to switch a game to a boys' pitch which has been too small. If a referee suspects that a playing area is too big, he should report it so that it can be checked. If the

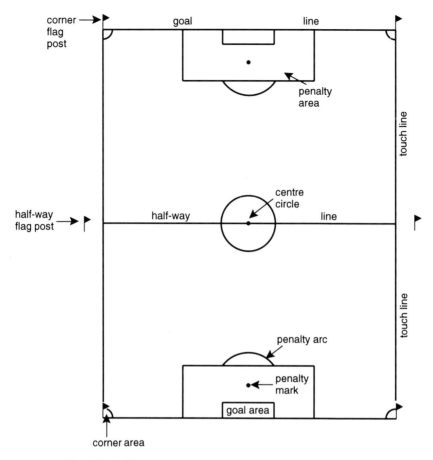

Fig. 17 The field of play

area is too small, he should refuse to play a competitive game. However, it is possible to play veterans matches (i.e. players over 35 years old) on playing areas which are smaller than those required by the laws.

The markings

The overall marking of the field of play should be clear and distinctive, and in lines which are not rutted. Ruts can be dangerous if players catch their ankles in them, and also tend to 'trap' the ball so that it runs along the rut where it would otherwise have clearly gone out of play. Obviously the lines should be distinctive, otherwise the decision as to whether the ball has gone out of play becomes a matter for guesswork. Sometimes the lines become indistinct, due either to bad weather or, more frequently, the club not having bothered to re-mark the field after the previous week's game. If necessary, and if practicable, ask the club to re-mark where required so that mistakes are less likely to occur.

At each corner of the field there must be a corner flag, mounted on a vertical post. Each post should stand at least 5 feet above the ground, and have a non-pointed top. The reason for this is simple: if a tall player falls on to a post that is less than 5 feet it is likely to hit him in the chest, possibly injuring his ribs.

Half-way flags may be placed on the half-way line, and at least a yard outside the touch-line, but these are not compulsory.

The centre circle

In the centre of the field a mark is made for the kick-off, or 'place kick'. From this a circle is drawn with a radius of 10 yards, known as the 'centre circle'. The purpose of this is to enable the referee to ensure that the opposing team are standing at least 10 yards from the ball at the kick-off.

The goal area

The goal area, or '6-yard box', is produced by measuring 6 yards from the inside of each goal post along the goal line, and from that point marking a 6-yard line into the field of play at right angles to the goal line. These lines are then connected by a line parallel to the goal line. The purpose of the goal areas is threefold.

(1) To show where a goal kick should be taken from.
(2) To show the area within which the goalkeeper is entitled to some greater protection. (This is covered in Law 12.)
(3) To show where a free kick, awarded for an offence within the goal area, should be taken from.

The penalty area

The penalty area is produced by measuring 18 yards from the inside of the goal posts, and then marking a line 18 yards into the field of play on each side of the goal. The purpose of the penalty area is threefold.

(1) To define the area within which the defending goalkeeper may handle the ball.
(2) To show when the ball is in play following a goal kick or a defending team's free kick taken within the penalty area.
(3) To show where, if one of the nine penal offences is committed by a defending player against an opponent while the ball is in play, the referee should award a penalty kick.

We will return to some of the points raised by this later in the course. Remember that the penalty area *includes* the lines which border it, so that offences committed *on* the line are said to be committed *within* the penalty area.

Within the penalty area is a mark known as the 'penalty spot'. This indicates the point from which a penalty kick should be taken. Experience shows that this mark is likely to be wrong or missing or indistinct in a high proportion of cases. On one occasion, I refereed a cup semi-final. On arriving at the ground, I inspected the field of play and discovered that one penalty spot was 14 and not 12 yards from the goal line. With plenty of time to spare, I was able to rectify this. A year later I was appointed to another cup semi-final on the same ground, and as I spoke to the linesmen while we walked around the pitch before the start of play, I told them of the previous year's incident. As we looked at one of the penalty areas, sure enough the same mistake had happened again! Fortunately, I had a long surveyor's tape with me and we were able to check the dimensions. It doesn't take too much imagination to realise the problems a referee would face in a critical game during which the penalty spot has to be re-positioned before the kick can be taken.

Finally, an arc is produced from the penalty spot. This is to show the minimum distance from the ball from which players must be when a penalty kick is taken.

The corner area

The other marking on the field which the law requires is the corner area. Here a small quarter-circle is drawn from the corner flag, and this simply shows the area within which the ball must be placed when a corner is to be taken.

The photographer's line

One other, optional, mark on the field is the 'photographer's line'. Usually, this is to be found at professional clubs where a large number of photographers are likely to congregate, and ensures that players are not distracted by flash bulbs and the close proximity of photographers. You may ask whether this has any real relevance to the average referee in a local game. Although an army of photographers is unlikely to turn up for the sort of games which most of us referee, it is often the case that a friend of a player, or an occasional local reporter or club official, will turn up to take a few pictures. If he gets in the way, then you can suggest that he moves back to roughly where the line would be, so that he doesn't cause a distraction.

Questions
(Answers on page 49.)

Question 4 Study the map of the field of play at the top of the next page and fill in the correct dimensions below.

(a) A–B .... (c) E–F ....
(b) A–D .... (d) E–N ....

Fig. 18 Fill in the correct dimensions

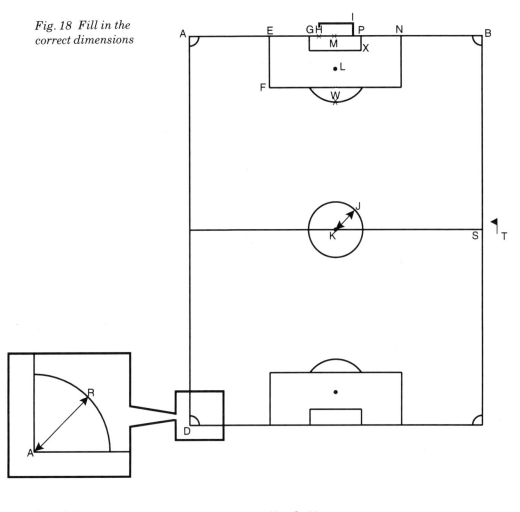

(e) H–I ....

(f) G–P ....

(g) K–J ....

(h) A–R ....

(i) S–T ....

(j) G–H ....

(k) P–X ....

(l) L–M ....

(m) L–W ....

Question 5 The goal and touch lines are considered not to be part of the field of play. True or false?

Question 6 When measuring along the goal line to mark out the 6- and 18-yard lines for the goal and penalty areas, from which point should the measurement be taken?

Question 7 What is the minimum height of a corner flag above the ground?

Question 8   What is the minimum width of a touch line?

Question 9   What is the maximum width of a touch line?

Question 10   Would you allow a game on a field of play with dimensions of 100 yards long by 50 yards wide?

Question 11   Is a penalty area of smaller size than stated in the laws acceptable?

Question 12   On a playing area of minimum width, how far will the edge of the penalty area be from the touch line?

Question 13   On a playing area of maximum width, how far will the edge of the penalty area be from the touch line?

The goals

We turn now to a crucial piece of equipment on the field of play, but at least the dimensions are easy to remember! The problem with the goal, and, more particularly the goal nets, is that any defect here can result in an otherwise legitimate goal being disallowed, or alternatively, an illegal one being given. So it is essential that the referee checks the goals very thoroughly for any weaknesses before the start of the game.

Questions
(Answers on page 49.)

Question 14   What are the dimensions of the goals?

Question 15   What shapes are permissible for goal posts?

Question 16   Are nets compulsory according to the laws?

Question 17   Is a cross-bar compulsory?

When the referee checks the nets prior to the game, he is looking for several things. The best way to show this is with an illustration.
(1) The net is properly pegged down at the sides and behind the goal, so that the ball cannot squeeze under it either into or out of the goal.
(2) The net doesn't sag and thus hinder the goalkeeper, and there are no large holes in the net.
(3) The net is properly attached to the cross-bar.
(4) The posts are upright and firm, so that the goal cannot rock backwards and forwards.
(5) The net is properly secured to the posts, so that the ball cannot enter the goal through the side netting and the players cannot be impeded.

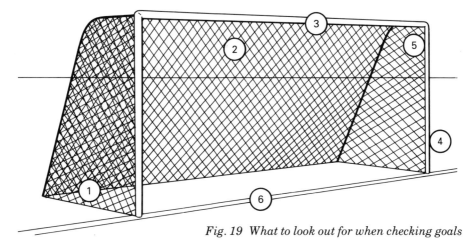

Fig. 19 What to look out for when checking goals

(6) The goal line is clearly and accurately marked, so that the referee has a good view if and when a goal is scored.

By now you may know that nets are not compulsory so far as the *laws* of soccer are concerned, but almost all leagues and cup competitions now require nets to be provided as part of the *rules* of the competition. When you inspect the goals, insist on the club putting right any defects which you have found.

Safety

The referee must give prime consideration to players' safety where the condition of the playing surface is concerned. Of course, if the pitch is covered by 2 feet of snow or 6 inches of flood water, then it will not only be dangerous but quite impossible to play. Between a snow- or ice-bound field and a normal playing surface is a grey area in which the referee must use his judgment in making a decision as to whether a game should start or not. Rutted and frozen grounds can be highly dangerous, as can grounds where a drain has failed, leading to a a small bog appearing in one part of the field through which it is impossible to move. It may be possible to visit a ground well before the game and make an early decision, thus stopping the away team from having to undertake a long and pointless journey. Sometimes a locally based referee will do this if the ground is some distance from where you live.

Part 2 _____
Law 2 – The ball

This law is quite simple and straightforward, but there are some important tips and useful advice which the referee will need. It is vital that a ball used in a match is of standard specification, and the law states what this specification is. Start by answering the following question.

Question
(Answer on page 49.)

Question 18 What are the five criteria to which a ball must conform to be acceptable?

Most balls used are made to standard weight and size, so this rarely causes a problem. But there are some training balls available of less than the regulation weight. As a ball ages its shape can become deformed, and a referee may find himself being offered such a ball for a game, which he should, of course, reject. The most common problem occurs with the pressure of the ball. Often, club secretaries will either pump it up like a cannon ball, or alternatively, it will be too soft. With a poorly organised junior club, it is not uncommon for the ball to be given to the referee at the kick-off, with the result that the game must be delayed if it needs to be inflated or deflated. Often, clubs fail to have the proper equipment to do this, which creates further problems.

A good tip here is to make sure that the ball is inspected well before the game starts. If possible, any spare balls which may be needed if the ball is kicked out of the ground should also be checked. After this, the referee should also make sure that he hangs on to it. Most importantly, don't forget to take it out on to the field with you!

Another piece of good advice is to take along an old pump and some valve adaptors. This will enable you to put things right quickly if the ball pressure needs to be changed. Remember that the pressure may vary quite a lot, and the ball may still remain acceptable within the laws.

Questions

(Answers on pages 49–50.)

Question 19 A player shoots towards goal and the ball hits the cross-bar. As it does so, it bursts. What should the referee do and how should he re-start the game?

Question 20 You arrive at a ground to discover that there are only three corner flags, and two of these are only 4 feet 6 inches high. The club tells you that they have no other corner flags available. What should you do?

Question 21 You inspect a ground before the kick-off on a very cold afternoon, finding that it is very hard and frosty. Although mostly flat and even, some ruts exist where a tractor has been driven on what was a muddy patch on the edge of the field by the half-way line, and this seems dangerous to you. The two teams are keen to play, and tell you that they will be happy to accept full responsibility for any injuries that occur if the game is played. What action should you take?

Question 22 You are advised to get to the ground in good time to check the field of play. How early do you think the referee should arrive at the ground?

Part 3 _____
Law 3 – Number of players

This law begins by stating simply that a team will normally consist of 11 players, one of whom shall be the goalkeeper.

Question

(Answer on page 50.)

Question 23 With 15 minutes of the game having been played, the referee notes that one team has 12 players in its side. What should the referee do?

Goalkeepers

The goalkeeper has special privileges in his own penalty area, and the person acting as goalkeeper must be clearly identified by wearing a distinctive jersey. The goalkeeper may change places with an outfield player provided this takes place:

(a) when the ball is out of play
(b) with the permission of the referee.

Occasionally, but fortunately not very often, the goalkeeper may change places with another player *without* the referee's permission.

Question

(Answer on page 50.)

Question 24 A goalkeeper changes places with a defender without having obtained the permission of the referee. He removes the goalkeeper's jersey but stops the ball with his hand inside the penalty area, with the defender's shirt partly on. The defender has put on the goalkeeper's jersey. What should the referee do?

Substitutes

In virtually every competition, substitutes are now permitted.

Question

(Answer on page 50.)

Question 25 What is the maximum number of substitutes allowed in a competitive game?

The procedure for making a substitution is as follows.

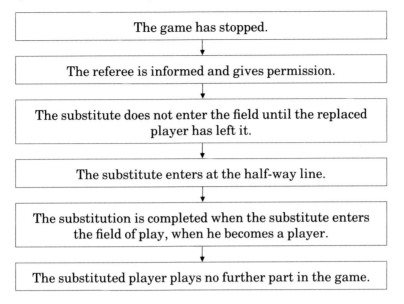

| The game has stopped. |
| The referee is informed and gives permission. |
| The substitute does not enter the field until the replaced player has left it. |
| The substitute enters at the half-way line. |
| The substitution is completed when the substitute enters the field of play, when he becomes a player. |
| The substituted player plays no further part in the game. |

Questions

(Answers on page 50.)

Question 26   During a stoppage in play, a team wishes to make a substitution. As the substitute is about to enter the field, but before play has re-started, the substituted player uses foul language to the referee. Should the referee allow the substitution to take place?

Question 27   In the second half of a match, and just after a goal has been scored, the referee realises that the scorer is a substitute who was not on the field in the first half and did not receive the referee's permission to play. What action should the referee take?

Finally, if a referee is really unlucky, he may come across the following problem.

Question 28   A player swears at the referee before the start of the game. The referee decides to send him off for foul language. Can he be substituted or must his team play with only ten players?

Part 4

The players' equipment

The compulsory equipment of a player consists of:

(a) jersey or shirt
(b) shorts
(c) stockings
(d) shinguards
(e) footwear

Note that very recently it has become necessary for players to wear shin-guards, and the referee is required to ensure that they do.

The main concern for the referee here is the safety of other players. It is important to make sure that players wear nothing that could be dangerous to themselves or other players.

Question
(Answer on page 50.)

Question 29 A player is wearing a large ring which the referee considers might be dangerous. What action should he take?

Frequently, a player's boots may be in a dangerous state, with sharp, burred edges on the studs. If this is the case, an otherwise harmless tackle may result in an injury. Many players also wear rings, necklaces and crucifixes. These may be dangerous. If the referee is unhappy with them, he should ask the player to remove them.

Question
(Answer on page 50.)

Question 30 What action should the referee take if a player complains that an opponent's footwear is dangerous?

It is important to remember that the players rely on the referee to do his best to ensure that the game is played safely. If he has any doubt, he has the right to inspect a player's footwear at any time.

Finally, in recent seasons the use of 'thermopants' or cycling shorts has grown. Players are allowed to use them, but they must be the same colour as the shorts the team is wearing. They must not extend further than the top of the knee. If a team is wearing multi-coloured shorts, the referee should judge whether the colour of the cycling shorts matches the *predominant* colour of the soccer shorts.

Answers

Question 1   100 and 130 yards.

Question 2   50 and 100 yards.

Question 3   Rectangular (the length must always exceed the breadth).

Question 4   (a) 50–100 yards; (b) 100–130 yards; (c) 18 yards; (d) 44 yards; (e) 8 yards; (f) 20 yards; (g) 10 yards; (h) 1 yard; (i) at least 1 yard; (j) 6 yards; (k) 6 yards; (l) 12 yards; (m) 10 yards.

Question 5   False.

Question 6   From the inside of the nearer goal post.

Question 7   5 feet.

Question 8   No minimum width is stipulated, but the lines should be clearly visible.

Question 9   5 inches.

Question 10   Yes.

Question 11   No, except in schoolchildren's games.

Question 12   3 yards.

Question 13   28 yards.

Question 14   8 yards wide by 8 feet high.

Question 15   Square, rectangular, round, half-round, elliptical.

Question 16   No, but they are normally required by the rules of the competition.

Question 17   Yes, in a competitive match a cross-bar is essential.

Question 18   Weight (14–16 ounces), size (27–28 inches circumference), shape (spherical), pressure (0.6–1.1 atmospheres), material (leather or other approved materials).

Question 19   Stop play. Re-start the game from where the ball became deflated with a dropped ball. If this is where the ball hit the cross-bar, the ball should be dropped at the nearest point on the edge of the goal area.

Question 20   Although the law states that corner flags must be used, it is possible to play a game without them. It is in the *spirit* of the laws of the game to discard the dangerous corner flags and to play without them.

Question 21 Do not play the game if you are unhappy about the safety of the ground. By refereeing the game you are accepting a high degree of responsibility.

Question 22 The referee is generally expected to be at the ground at least half-an-hour before the kick-off. Amongst other things, he needs to check the ball, sign any last-minute registration forms, and arrange his own kit and equipment before the start of play.

Question 23 Stop the game. If practicable, the referee should re-start the game from the beginning. After the match he should send a report to the appropriate authority.

Question 24 He should award a penalty. The defender, by putting the goalkeeper's jersey on, is now considered to be the 'keeper and has his privileges concerning handling the ball. The former 'keeper is now an outfield player and is not entitled to handle the ball. Both players should be cautioned for ungentlemanly conduct.

Question 25 Two, although these may be drawn from a maximum of five names.

Question 26 No. The player about to be substituted should be sent off for foul language, and a report submitted. For the substitute to now come on, another player would have to go off.

Question 27 The goal is allowed to stand, but the player should be cautioned for entering the field of play without permission. A good piece of advice here is to ask both sides at half-time if they have any substitutes on, and thus avoid having to caution players later for entering the field of play without permission.

Question 28 The player can be replaced by one of the named substitutes. Note that the team cannot now nominate another substitute.

Question 29 The referee should ask the player to take the ring off. An alternative is for the player to cover it with tape.

Question 30 When the ball is out of play, he should check the player's footwear. If he is unhappy with it, he should tell the player to leave the field to have it attended to. When the player has done this, at a stoppage in play he should check to make sure that his footwear is now safe. He does not need to report this.

Unit 3
Laws 7-11

Part 1
Law 7 – The duration of play

The law states that a game should consist of two equal periods, normally of 45 minutes each. Under certain circumstances, such as fading light, the rules of the competition under which the game is being played may allow for it to be shorter than this, usually 40 or 35 minutes each way.

Question
(Answer on page 66.)

Question 1 In an evening match, the referee plays 45 minutes in the first half but notices that the light is fading fast in the interval. Since the rules of the competition allow for games to last a total of 80 minutes, can he now play a second half of 35 minutes?

The laws give players a right to a half-time break; but this should not be greater than 5 minutes. Sometimes, when the weather is cold and miserable, and there is nowhere for players to shelter, everyone prefers to turn straight round at half-time and kick off for the second half. However, players have a right to a half-time break, and they can take one if they so choose.

Question
(Answer on page 66.)

Question 2 When is time (a) 'extended' and (b) 'allowed' in a match?

During a game, stoppages are likely to occur. Injuries, the loss of a ball, a sudden hailstorm or a floodlight failure are among many possible causes of the game being temporarily halted. If this occurs, the referee is required to allow time to be added to ensure that the game still lasts the full 90 minutes.

It is possible that the referee will award a penalty just before the end of the first or second half. If this occurs, the referee must *extend* time to allow the kick to be taken or re-taken. This is dealt with again in Unit 5.

Question
(Answer on page 66.)

Question 3   If the referee abandons the match due to the elements or other cause, what does he *not* have the power to decide?

Part 2 _____

Law 8 – The start of play

The law allows for captains to have the choice of ends or the kick-off by the toss of a coin.

Question
(Answer on page 66.)

Question 4 What action should the referee take if the players refuse to shake hands just before the toss of the coin to decide kick-off or choice of ends?

The captain winning the toss can opt for the kick-off rather than choice of ends: this means that the other captain must make a decision as to which end his team has. This can be disconcerting to the other side and is sometimes used as a deliberate tactic by an experienced captain to 'throw' the opposition a little. Incidentally, it is necessary to toss for choice of ends or kick-off after 90 minutes, if extra time is being played.

Question
(Answer on page 66.)

Question 5 Where must all the players be located at the kick-off?

When the kick-off is taken, the players must be correctly positioned before the ball is in play. Therefore, the referee should position himself so that he is in a good location to view any encroachment that might occur. Opponents cannot come within 10 yards of the ball, or into the opponents' half, until it is kicked, *not* when the whistle is blown.

The ball must go *forwards* at the kick-off. If it does not, the referee must insist that the kick be re-taken. As with other kicks to re-start the game, the ball must travel its own circumference before being in play, and it should not be touched by another player until it has done so.

Question
(Answer on page 66.)

Question 6 At the kick-off the ball rolls its own circumference, but it is then kicked a second time by the player who kicked off. What action should the referee take?

A kick-off or place kick is taken to start each half of the game, or each half of extra time when this is being played. It is used also to re-start the game after a goal has been scored.

At times the game has to be stopped by the referee when the ball is in play, as when a player is injured or if the ball deflates. When this occurs, the referee re-starts the game with a dropped ball from the place where the ball was situated when play was stopped. The referee should drop the ball from about waist height. As soon as it touches the ground, it is in play.

Questions

(Answers on page 66.)

Question 7 The referee re-starts play with a dropped ball but a player kicks the ball before it has touched the ground. What action should the referee take?

Question 8 How many players are allowed to be involved when the referee re-starts play with a dropped ball?

The dropped ball is a good reminder of the danger to the referee of keeping the whistle in his mouth when the game in in progress. There is always a chance that the ball will be kicked upwards towards the referee's face, and this may cause him to suffer a serious facial injury, with the whistle being driven through his teeth.

Part 3 _____
Law 9 – Ball in and out of play

The law states that the ball is said to be 'out of play' in one of two circumstances.

(1) When the ball has wholly crossed the line, either on the ground or in the air.

(2) When the game has been stopped by the referee.

At all other times the ball is in play, including when it rebounds off the posts, cross-bar, corner flags or the referee.

Question
(Answer on page 66.)

Question 9 The ball is about to go out of play over the touch line, but rebounds off the linesman who is standing just inside the field of play. What action should the referee take?

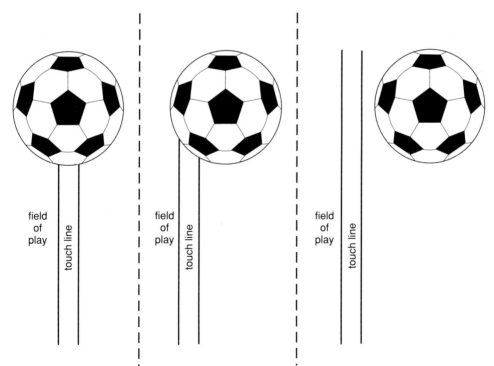

Fig. 20 Left – ball in play; centre – ball in play; right – ball out of play

For the ball to be out of play when it crosses over the goal or touch lines, the *whole* of the ball must go out of play. Since the lines are part of the field of play, so long as a *part* of the ball is in line with the markings, it is said to be still in play. Frequently this is not understood by players and managers at all levels. This can be seen in the diagram on the previous page.

Question

(Answer on page 67.)

Question 10   The ball rebounds into play from a half-way-line flag. What is the referee's decision?

Part 4 _____

Law 10 – Method of scoring

The law states that, for a goal to be awarded, the *whole* of the ball must cross the line, either on the ground or in the air, between the goal posts and under the cross-bar.

Questions

(Answers on page 67.)

Question 11   Under what circumstances can a goal be scored when the ball has been thrown into the goal?

Question 12   Can a goal be scored direct from (a) a goal kick; (b) a place kick; (c) a defending player's free kick into his own goal; (d) a corner kick?

It is important for the referee to bear in mind that it is impossible to award a goal if the ball has not *wholly* crossed the line. If, for example, a spectator or a dog or a ball from another game, comes on to the field, makes contact with the ball and prevents a certain goal, then the referee must stop the game and re-start with a dropped ball.

Part 5 _____

Law 11 – Offside

Although the offside law is very brief, it has proved one of the most difficult and controversial for referees to enforce. This is due to several reasons. Firstly, in recent years the game has become steadily faster, and this makes judging offside much more difficult. The linesman must be continually moving along the touch line to maintain a position in line with the last-but-one defender or the most advanced attacker – this requires considerable concentration.

Secondly, in recent times the offside law has become an important element of the tactics of a team, with defenders deliberately forcing attackers towards the middle of the field by moving up together. This has meant that offside decisions are critical to the result of the game, and form the basis of endless post-match debate. Even at the highest level, linesmen have been shown to make crucial errors in judgment when the game is moving rapidly.

Thirdly, the law contains the following words which place considerable pressure on the referee: . . . *if, in the opinion of the referee, he* [the player in question] *is (a) interfering with play or with an opponent, or (b) seeking to gain an advantage by being in that offside position.* In other words, just being in an offside position is not sufficient to be judged offside. The referee has to make up his mind that the player is interfering, with play or with an opponent, or seeking to gain an advantage, before he gives a free kick for offside.

For a player to be offside, initially he must be:

(1) in his opponents' half, and
(2) in front of the ball, i.e. he must be between the ball and the opponents' goal line.

Thus a player cannot be judged offside if he is in his own half, or if he is behind the ball when it is played.

Question
(Answer on page 67.)

Question 13   What is the punishment for offside?

    Assuming that the player fulfils the two conditions above, he can be judged offside if *at the moment the ball is played* he has less than two defenders between himself and the opponents' goal line.

In the diagram below the attacking player (A) has kicked the ball forwards to a colleague (B). Clearly, player B is in an offside position when the ball is played, and he is seeking to gain an advantage and interfering with play. The referee should thus penalise player B for being offside.

If player B has at least two defenders between him and the goal line at some point *after* the ball has been kicked, this makes no difference to the decision.

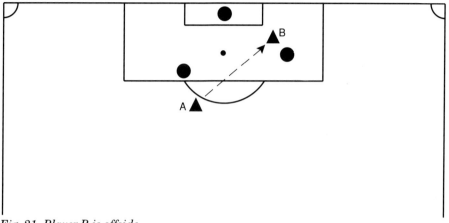

Fig. 21 Player B is offside

Player A in the diagram below passes the ball forwards to player B. Player B runs forwards when the ball is kicked, and receives it in a position a few yards behind the two defenders. He is not offside because there were two defenders between him and the goal line when the ball was played.

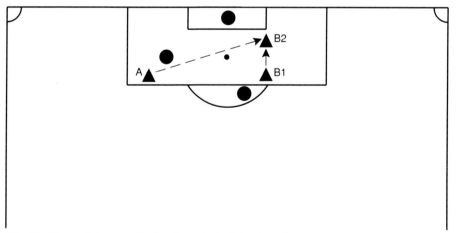

Fig. 22 Player B is not offside when the ball is played

In the next diagram the attacker, player B, runs back to receive the ball. Note that the player was offside when the ball was played, and since this is when offside is judged, the referee should penalise the attacker.

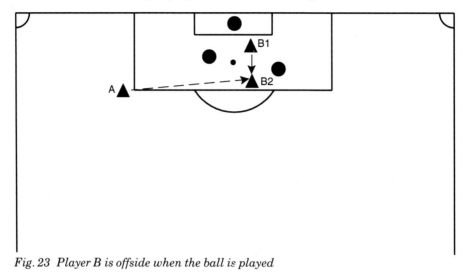

Fig. 23 Player B is offside when the ball is played

For the 1990-1 season, the offside law changed in one important detail. Now a player cannot be judged offside if he is *in line with* the last-but-one defender.

In the diagram below player A passes the ball to player B, who is in line with the last-but-one defender. Because he is in line with that player, he is not offside.

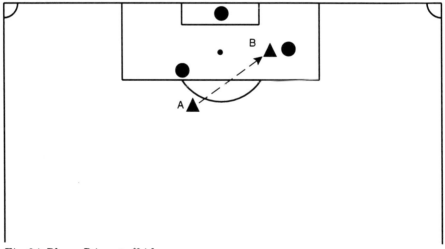

Fig. 24 Player B is not offside

In each of these cases, where the player has been judged offside he is clearly interfering with play or seeking to gain an advantage. In practice, making this judgment is more complicated because on many occasions the player may be remote from the action and thus not interfering with play. A few examples can illustrate this problem.

Study the next diagram. Here, attacking player A passes the ball forwards to player B, who is clearly in an onside position. The colleague in the outside right position, player C, is clearly offside. Should the referee penalise the attacking team for offside? Most referees in this position would claim that player C was not interfering, or seeking to gain an advantage, but this depends on several factors. Has he taken a defender with him out to the wing? Is he near to the goal line and thus distracting the goalkeeper? Clearly, if the answer to these questions is yes, then the referee is more likely to penalise the forward. The problem is, where does the referee draw the line? If the player is only 15 yards into his opponents' half, the situation is different from if he is only 20 yards from the goal line. If he is 5 yards from the touch line, this again is different from being 10 yards from it.

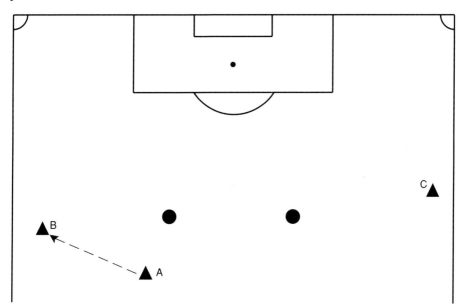

Fig. 25 When player A passes to B, should the referee penalise player C for being in an offside position, i.e. is he interfering with play or seeking to gain an advantage?

Questions

(Answers on page 67.)

Question 14 Can a player be adjudged offside from: (a) a goal kick; (b) a corner kick; (c) a throw-in; (d) an indirect free kick taken from inside his own penalty area; (e) a direct free kick awarded to his side; (f) an opposing player's back pass?

Question 15 The referee waves play on because he does not consider an offside player to be interfering with play or seeking to gain an advantage. The player who received the ball kicks for goal and the ball rebounds to the player who was offside, who now shoots for goal. What should the referee do?

Another, similar situation occurs when a player shoots for goal from a long distance, with a colleague standing in an offside position.

In the diagram below, player A shoots at goal from a position 35 yards from goal. His colleague (B) is a yard offside. Should the referee penalise him for being offside? In this situation most referees would claim that the player should not be penalised for being offside, unless he had distracted the defender nearby or the goalkeeper. In the next situation, however, the circumstances are rather more difficult.

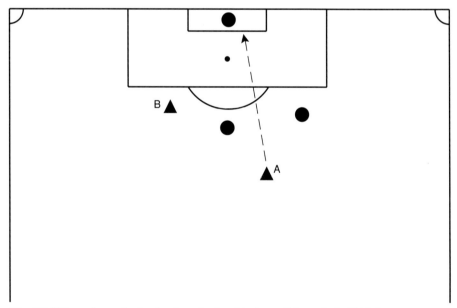

Fig. 26 When player A shoots at goal, should player B be ruled offside?

Study the next diagram (below). As the offside attacking player (B) moves nearer and nearer to the goal, so it is more likely that he will be considered to be interfering with play. Here I am sure that most referees would give offside against him.

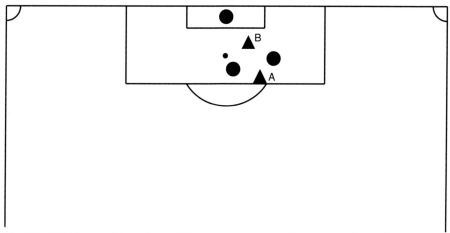

Fig. 27 Offside attacking player (B) moving nearer and nearer to the goal

The next diagram (below) shows that the attacking player (A) has chipped the ball past the defender on his way to goal. His attacking colleague (B) is in an offside position. Offside can only be given when the ball is released. Therefore, if the attacking player retains control of the ball when dribbling it past a defender, it would be wrong to give offside be-

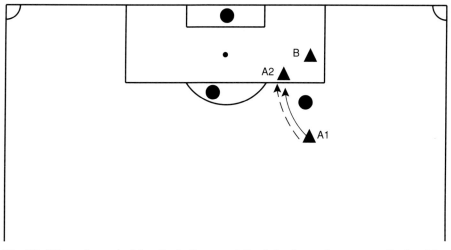

Fig. 28 When player A chips the ball around the defender and runs on to it, should player B be ruled offside?

cause the ball has *not* been released. This can be difficult to judge if the attacker kicks the ball in the air about 20 yards forwards and chases on to it. Although the ball may not be played by the attacking player who is offside, but is played on by the original player, the referee must decide whether the second player is interfering with play. After all, the ball has been released by the attacker, even though he intends to and succeeds in regaining control of it. Once again, the referee must make his mind up, quickly and under pressure.

In the next situation (*see* diagram below), two players have broken through the defence. Player A shoots for goal. Should the referee penalise player B for being offside? Since player B is not seeking to interfere with play or an opponent, he should not be penalised and the goal should be allowed to stand.

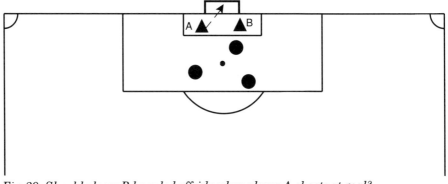

Fig. 29 Should player B be ruled offside when player A shoots at goal?

Occasionally, a player will place himself in an offside position at a penalty kick. This is shown in the diagram below. Player A is going to take the penalty kick, and his colleague, player B, is in an offside position. Should the referee penalise the offside attacker? In this situation, the

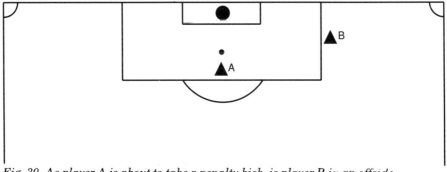

Fig. 30 As player A is about to take a penalty kick, is player B in an offside position?

referee should not penalise the offside player unless the ball rebounds from the goal, and he subsequently becomes involved in the play. My advice is to go over to the offside player and warn him that, if he becomes involved in play, he will be penalised for offside. Usually, this will be enough to encourage him to stand elsewhere.

Using the linesmen

Briefing the linesmen has already been discussed in general terms in Unit 1. Of course, the linesman's job is particularly important in judging offside. Only by being exactly square to the most advanced attacker or last-but-one defender can the linesman properly judge offside. In refereeing local matches, the referee has to depend on club linesmen, and here the quality of support he receives can vary considerably. A good linesman can make a game flow well, with players having confidence in his signals, and the referee able to delegate offside to him and thus concentrate on other aspects of the game.

Quite often, however, the linesman has little interest in the job at all. Sometimes he may be the substitute, more interested in getting on the field than watching from the side lines. Sometimes he is the team secretary, trainer, treasurer and everything else rolled into one. Therefore, his mind may not always be on the job in hand. Finally, there is the well meaning but elderly volunteer who has trouble in keeping in position. A friend of mine was in charge of a local junior game. Frustrated at the linesman's inability to keep up with play, he went to speak to him to suggest that he try to move a little more quickly. The linesman indignantly retorted that he couldn't be expected to move any more quickly 'at my age'. In general, perhaps it is preferable to have such a linesman rather than none at all, and this is often the only option.

When briefing the club linesman, I usually try to involve him in the game as much as I can. When he gives offside, I tell him to stay with his flag raised until I acknowledge his signal. If I can play advantage then I will, but otherwise I will generally go with the linesman unless I feel strongly that he is wrong. On occasion it takes a few seconds for me to look over to the linesman. I remember once looking over to see if the linesman was giving offside and because I had taken my eyes off the game for two seconds, I missed a blatant handball in the penalty area. I learned from this lesson: now I warn the linesman that he may be waving his flag for a while, but ask him to stand his ground until I have clearly signalled to him. Failing to acknowledge the linesman can lead to him becoming demoralised and he may lose interest, so don't forget!

From time to time, a team will provide a weak linesman and insist on playing the offside trap. This is very hard for the referee. My advice here is to talk to the team captain, and gently suggest that in the circumstances playing an offside trap may not be a very good idea, because errors are almost bound to occur.

Among all the laws, offside is without doubt one of the most difficult for a referee to apply consistently. The higher speed of the game, the deliberate use of 'offside trap' tactics, poor support from linesmen, and an emphasis on the 'referee's opinion' in judging offside, make it a tough law to apply well. Experience and fitness can go a long way in helping a referee to become proficient at applying offside. Often, referees claim that 'A dodgy offside is better than a dodgy goal', but no referee should be happy with a situation in which a team may have been unfairly denied a good goal.

Answers

Question 1   The law states clearly that the game should be of two *equal* periods. The referee cannot, therefore, play a 45-minute half followed by a 35-minute half. If in any doubt, the referee should err on the side of caution and play less time in the first half.

Question 2   Time should be *extended,* according to the laws, only so that the taking of a penalty kick can be completed. Time should be *allowed* where it has been lost earlier in the game due to injury, substitutions, bad weather or other disruption.

Question 3   The referee does not have the power to decide the result of the game. This is out of his hands altogether.

Question 4   No action can be taken here. The captains are under no obligation to shake hands before the start of play.

Question 5   At the kick-off, the players should be in their own half of the field of play, and in the case of the side not kicking the game off, should be at least 10 yards from the ball. The players must remain in these positions until the ball is kicked.

Question 6   Once the ball has rolled its own circumference, it is in play. If the kicker now plays the ball a second time, the referee should award an indirect free kick to the opposing team.

Question 7   The ball cannot be played until it has touched the ground. The referee should stop play and re-start by re-taking the dropped ball.

Question 8   The law does not make reference to the number of players who can be involved with a dropped ball. The convention is that one of each side challenges for the ball, but there is no stipulation that this should be so.

Question 9   No action should be taken. The linesman is part of the game, and play continues if the ball rebounds from him within the field of play.

Question 10   Since the half-way-line flag must be at least a yard from the touch line, the ball has gone out of play and the referee should award a throw-in.

Question 11   Only when thrown by the attacking team's goalkeeper from his own penalty area, or thrown into the goal by the defending team's goalkeeper.

Question 12   (a) No; (b) no; (c) no – a goal cannot be scored direct into a player's own goal from a free kick of any description; (d) yes.

Question 13   The punishment for offside is an indirect free kick to the non-offending side from the place where the player was standing when he was judged offside. If the offside was judged to have occurred in the goal area, the free kick can be taken from anywhere within the area.

Question 14   (a) No; (b) no; (c) no; (d) yes; (e) yes; (f) no. Note that players cannot be offside if they receive the ball direct from a goal kick. Many teams are unaware of this, so that opponents place themselves in an offside position at a goal kick to take advantage of their ignorance.

Question 15   Now that the player *has* sought an advantage, he can be penalised for offside. This is a problem area for the referee, who can find himself having to give an offside decision some time after the original offside.

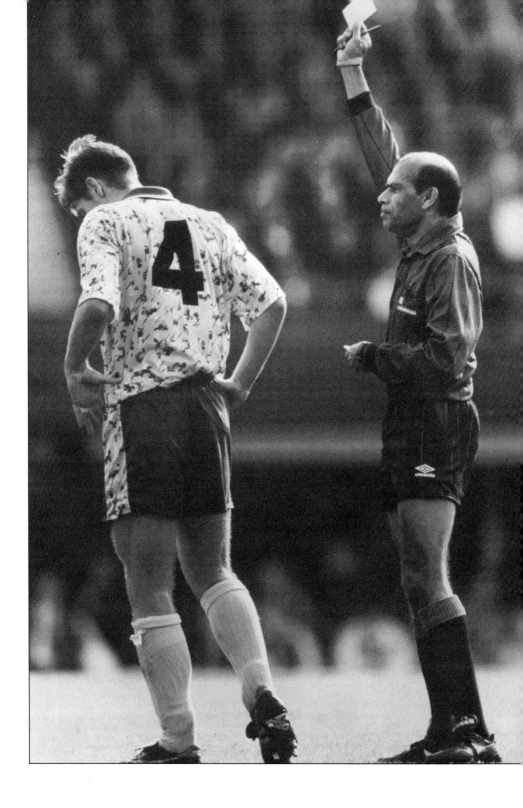

Unit 4
Fouls and misconduct

A well-known coach once said that the laws of soccer were quite simple: 'If it moves kick it. If it doesn't move, kick it 'til it does'. In the minds of some players, perhaps this is not so far from the truth. Like any other sport, soccer reflects the society it is played in. The greater problems of man-management and match control created by a more aggressive society are ones which the referee must come to terms with. This unit will consider the various offences which players might commit, and the way in which the referee should deal with them.

Part 1
The penal offences

The laws indicate that penal offences – those committed intentionally by a player on an opponent while the ball is in play – should be penalised by a direct free kick. The free kick should take place at the position where the incident occurred.

If such an offence occurs within the penalty area and the offence is committed by a defender on an attacker, then a penalty should be awarded.

Question
(Answer on page 97.)

Question 1   A player deliberately kicks an opponent within his own penalty area while the ball is in play in the other half of the field of play. What should the referee do?

(A) Kicking or attempting to kick an opponent

If a player makes no attempt to play the ball, but deliberately kicks an opponent, the referee should award a direct free kick or, where appropriate, a penalty kick to the opposition. Note that the kick does not have to make contact for this to happen. An *attempted* kick is sufficient for the referee to take action. The essential factor here is that the player *inten-*

tionally aims to kick an opponent. If the opponent is kicked in the process of a player making a fair tackle in which the ball is played clearly, the player should not be penalised.

Fig. 31 Kicking an opponent

Occasionally, a player lifts his studs and goes 'over the ball' in a tackle. This is a particularly dangerous tackle in which the opponent can suffer a serious injury if the tackler makes contact. If the referee sees this occur, and believes that the player has committed the act intentionally, then he should take action, usually by sending off the player (according to the severity of the offence).

(B) Tripping

A tripping offence is often committed by a player when all hope of making contact with the ball has gone, and his only hope is to bring down the opponent unfairly. Once again, the referee must judge whether the player *intended* to trip the opponent. Tripping refers not just to the use of the leg or foot, but also to the use of the body by stooping either behind or in front of the opponent.

Fig. 32 Tripping, by stooping in front of (or behind) an opponent

Fig. 33 Tripping, using the legs

(C) Jumping at an opponent

A player may jump at an opponent in a number of ways. He may, for example, jump with both feet at the opponent. It is also possible for the player to jump at the opponent using his whole body, knocking him over or forcing him off the ball in the process.

(D) Charging in a violent or dangerous manner

It is possible to quite legally charge an opponent but only when the ball is in playing distance, when both players are trying to play the ball, and when the charge is made shoulder to shoulder. If the charge is violent, involving excessive force, then the player should be penalised. A dangerous charge occurs when it is directed against a different part of the opponent's body, such as the middle of the back. Such a charge, even if applied with minimal force, is likely to knock the opponent off-balance at best, and, at worst, cause some physical injury.

Fig. 34 Fair charge

Fig. 35 Charge in the back

Fig. 36 Charging in a violent or dangerous manner

(E) Charging an opponent from behind in a violent or dangerous manner

As we have seen already, a player may not charge an opponent in the small of the back. It *is* possible to charge an opponent from behind if the opponent is obstructing him, but only if the charge is broadly aimed at the shoulder area of the opponent. If the opponent is *not* obstructing the player, he may not be charged in this way.

(F) Striking or attempting to strike an opponent, or spitting at him

As with kicking or attempting to kick an opponent, the player does not have to actually make contact in order for a free kick to be awarded for this offence. A wild swing is sufficient for the referee to award a direct free kick or, when appropriate, a penalty kick. In the case of a player spitting at an opponent, not only should a direct free kick or penalty kick be awarded, but the player should also be sent off for violent conduct. Frequently, the referee will send a player off for striking an opponent, because this is normally construed as violent conduct.

Fig. 37 Striking or attempting to strike an opponent

Question
(Answer on page 97.)

Question 2 A corner is taken. With the ball in the air above the penalty area, a defender and an attacker roll over the goal line into the goal where the defender punches the attacker and the attacker retaliates by head-butting him. What action should the referee take, and how should he re-start the game?

(G) Holding an opponent

In desperation, a player might hold an opponent by grabbing his shirt or arm, but holding can occur in other ways. For example, with both players on the floor following a tackle, a player might grip the opponent's ankle or his legs to prevent him from getting up and playing the ball. Another example is where a forward puts his arm out, apparently to steady himself, but holds his opponent off to gain an unfair advantage by stopping him from tackling fairly for the ball.

Fig. 38 Pulling an opponent's shirt – a holding offence

(H) Pushing an opponent

Frequently, a player will push an opponent in order to stop him from playing, or competing for, the ball. A player might attempt to hide such a push from behind, and it may be hard for the referee to spot, particularly if the players are close together and the ball is being kicked into play from a goal kick, for example. The referee is advised to stand square to the players in this situation so that he can judge whether this offence is occurring.

Fig. 39 Pushing an opponent

(I) Handling the ball

This law requires a very careful consideration of *intent*. Outfield players may frequently handle the ball, but if this is done unintentionally there is no need for the referee to penalise the player. Intentional handball is often described as 'hand to ball'; unintentional handball is described as 'ball to hand'. Of course, it is often very difficult to judge this precisely: a grey area occurs where the referee has to make up his mind as to whether the player has *intentionally* handled the ball.

Question
(Answer on page 97.)

Question 3 A player is sitting in his own penalty area putting his boot back on. The ball is kicked towards goal by an opponent, whereupon the player lifts his boot and re-directs the ball over the bar. What action should the referee take?

Remember that the goalkeeper is allowed to handle the ball within his own penalty area.

Questions
(Answers on page 97.)

Question 4 The goalkeeper, standing outside his own penalty area, reaches out and handles the ball inside his own penalty area. What action should the referee take?

Question 5 The goalkeeper, standing inside the penalty area, reaches outside the area and handles the ball. What action should the referee now take?

Question 6 A player commits unintentional handball, and then gains an advantage as the ball bounces kindly for him. What action should the referee take?

Where handball offences occur, they must be punished by the award of a direct free kick or a penalty kick. In addition to this, the referee might consider cautioning or sending off the offending player.

Question
(Answer on page 97.)

Question 7 A player commits a penal offence by deliberately tripping an opponent in the penalty area. The penalty is scored. Does this cancel out the need for the referee to take the offending player's name and report him for misconduct?

It is important to commit to memory the nine penal offences. An easier way to remember is to group them in the following way.

(A) Kicking or attempting to kick an opponent.
(B) Tripping an opponent. } committed
(C) Jumping at an opponent. } with the feet

(D) Charging an opponent in a violent
or dangerous manner.

(E) Charging an opponent from behind unless the
player is being obstructed.

} committed
with the body

(F) Striking, attempting to strike, or spitting
at an opponent.

(G) Holding an opponent.

(H) Handling the ball intentionally.

(I) Pushing an opponent.

} committed
with the hands

Part 2

Non-penal offences

There are several offences for which the correct award is an indirect free kick, i.e. a kick from which a goal *cannot* be scored direct, but must be played by another player first.

(A) Dangerous play

This is defined as play which, while in itself not against the spirit of the game, is dangerous to an opponent. A good example of this is when a player attempts to kick a ball at shoulder height. If no opponent is near him, this action would not be dangerous. However, if an opponent was attempting to play the ball with his head, behaviour which would be reasonable if it was at that height, the action by the player would be dangerous, and would unfairly distract the opponent. This is illustrated below.

Fig. 40 Dangerous play

If this occurs, the referee should award an indirect free kick to the non-offending side.

Occasionally, some incident may occur when the ball is at about waist height. What action should the referee take here? Since it is reasonable to attempt to kick the ball at this height, and similarly reasonable to attempt to head it, it is problematical to award a free kick for dangerous play in this situation.

What about when the ball is only a couple of feet off the ground and a player who has just fallen over now tries to head it?

Question
(Answer on page 97.)

Question 8   What action should the referee take in this case?

Other forms of dangerous play can occur. For example, the goalkeeper may be coming out to collect the ball and is challenged by an attacker. While the attacker can reasonably attempt to play the ball, if he launches himself at it when the goalkeeper is near he places the latter in considerable danger. Once again, an indirect free kick should be awarded.

Finally, the goalkeeper runs out and raises his leg to put off an attacker. Often a goalkeeper will raise his leg to improve his balance or to gain height, but if he does so to deter an attacker from challenging for the ball, then he should be penalised.

(B) Fair shoulder charge while the ball is not within playing distance

Provided the ball is within playing distance, a player is entitled to shoulder charge an opponent fairly. This means that the charge is delivered with his shoulder to the shoulder region of the opponent, and not carried out in a violent manner. If two players are running towards the ball and one shoulder charges the other before they are in playing distance of the ball, the referee should award an indirect free kick. The term 'playing distance' means that distance within which a player could stretch out his leg to make contact with the ball.

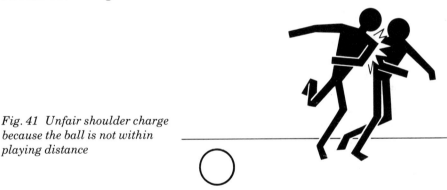

Fig. 41 Unfair shoulder charge because the ball is not within playing distance

(C) Obstruction

Obstruction is defined in the laws as: . . . *running between the opponent and the ball, or interposing the body so as to form an obstacle to an opponent.* It is perfectly reasonable, however, for a player to put his body between the opponent and the ball if the ball remains within playing distance.

If the ball is *not* within playing distance, the player is guilty of obstruction. Often, a player who has failed to win a tackle might obstruct an opponent in desperation. On occasion, if a ball is passed through towards the goalkeeper, a defender might obstruct an opponent to stop him from challenging fairly for the ball.

Obstruction might deny the opponent a clear opportunity to score a goal. When this occurs, despite the fact that only an indirect free kick is awarded, the referee will have to send off the offending player. This scenario is dealt with later in this unit.

Fig. 42 Obstruction

(D) Charging the goalkeeper

It is possible to shoulder charge the goalkeeper fairly, provided he is outside the goal area and is not holding the ball or obstructing an opponent. In practice, it is very rare for the goalkeeper to attempt to play the ball with his feet in this situation, and thus this type of incident is unusual. In the past, it was more acceptable for the goalkeeper to be shoulder charged by an attacking player while holding the ball.

(E) Goalkeeper not releasing the ball into play properly

Over the past few years the law has been changed several times in an attempt to ensure that goalkeepers do not waste time but release the ball into play quickly. This changing of the law has led to some confusion on the part of players and club officials, making the referee's role more difficult.

(i) Once the goalkeeper takes control of the ball with his hands, he can only take up to four steps with the ball before kicking or throwing it into play

Recently, some goalkeepers have developed the habit of retreating two paces before going forwards four steps. This means that they have taken a total of six steps before releasing the ball into play, an action which should be penalised by the award of an indirect free kick to the other side from where the offence occurred. The law now requires referees to be more firm in their interpretation of the goalkeeper gaining control with his hands. If the 'keeper parries a shot and then dives on the loose ball to pick it up, he now has four steps in which to move before he has to release it.

Questions
(Answers on page 98.)

Question 9   The ball is headed to the goalkeeper by a colleague. What action should the referee take?

Question 10   The ball is kicked back to the goalkeper by one of his colleagues. What action should the referee take if the goalkeeper: (a) picks the ball up; (b) plays the ball with his feet.

In an effort to reduce defensive play, it is now against the law for a goalkeeper to pick up the ball when it has been deliberately passed with the feet by a colleague. Note that passing the ball is not, in itself, an offence, but picking it up is, and should be penalised by the award of an indirect free kick from where the offence occurred. It is normally perfectly acceptable for a player to head or chest the ball to his goalkeeper. If however, this is done to get round the law, for example with one defender chipping the ball up in the air, and another heading it on to the goalkeeper, then this is an offence. The defender should be penalised, and an indirect free kick awarded against him from the place where the offence occurred. In this case, the offending player should be cautioned for ungentlemanly conduct.

(ii) The goalkeeper should not hold on to the ball for an unreasonable time before releasing it into play

The goalkeeper is not allowed to remain with the ball in his hands and unreasonably delay the game by failing to throw or kick the ball into play. If he does this, it is impossible for an opponent to challenge fairly for the ball, and the referee should award an indirect free kick to the opponents.

Question
(Answer on page 98.)

Question 11   The goalkeeper receives a pass from a colleague and dribbles the ball across the edge of the penalty area. An opponent complains to the referee that the goalkeeper is wasting time and should be penalised by the award of an indirect free kick. What action, if any, should the referee take?

The 'professional foul' – unfairly denying a goalscoring opportunity

In an attempt to penalise cynical, unfair play and to crack down on cheating, the laws have become much tougher on this type of offence in recent years. A player who is facing an open goal and an excellent goalscoring opportunity, receives a lesser award if he is given a free kick or a penalty following a so-called 'professional foul' which robs him of his chance on goal. Similarly, if a player deliberately handles the ball to deny a good goalscoring opportunity, the referee is required to take firm action against the player. This can be summarised as follows.

(a) An attacking player is fouled by an opponent and in the referee's opinion is denied a goalscoring opportunity.
Action   The player shall be sent off the field of play for the offence of serious foul play.
(b) A defender deliberately handles the ball, in an attempt to stop an obvious goalscoring opportunity.
Action   (i) If a goal is *not* scored, send the player off for serious foul play.
(ii) If a goal *is* scored, despite the defender's action, caution the player concerned.

It is important to remember that the judgment of the referee is crucial here. It is up to him to decide that a clear goalscoring opportunity has been spoiled. If it has, then he *must* send the offending player off. If it has not, then he may send off or caution the offending player, according to his judgment of the severity of the foul.

Part 3 _____
Other offences

So far we have considered offences committed by players on opponents, or by the goalkeeper when in possession of the ball. There are other offences which may occur in a game where the offending player has not committed an offence against an opponent, but where the referee has to penalise. In these cases, the correct way to re-start the game is normally with an indirect free kick.

(A) An assault by a player on a colleague, official or spectator

Occasionally, players from the same side will come into conflict. If this happens, the referee may have to stop the game to send off or caution the players concerned. When he has done this, he should re-start the game with an indirect free kick to the non-offending side, to be taken from where the incident occurred. From time to time a spectator may come on to the pitch and conflict occurs, in which case the referee should again deal with the player(s) concerned and re-start with an indirect free kick. If a linesman or the referee is assaulted, then once again an indirect free kick is the correct way to re-start the game. Remember, however, that if the referee is assaulted, it may be unwise to re-start the game if he has suffered injury or shock. This problem is dealt with later in this unit.

Question
(Answer on page 98.)

Question 12   A player leaves the field of play, and while the game is continuing, assaults a spectator. What action should the referee take and how should the game be re-started?

(B) An act of ungentlemanly conduct

Sometimes a player will commit an offence which will give his team an unfair advantage, and where the referee needs to penalise his team for this. There are several situations where this might occur.

(i) Distracting the opposition by calling for the ball

Occasionally a player will shout 'My ball!' or 'Leave it!' when attempting to gain control of the ball. Opponents may be confused by this and decide not to challenge for the ball. It is rarely a *deliberate* ploy by the player, but it may give an unfair advantage. This is classed as ungentlemanly conduct and, if play has been stopped, it should be re-started by the award of an indirect free kick if the referee considers that a team has gained an unfair advantage. If the referee considers that the player is *deliberately* trying to distract the opposition, then he should caution the player concerned for ungentlemanly conduct.

Sometimes a player will simply shout or yell in an attempt to distract an opponent. This represents ungentlemanly conduct and should be punished by the award of an indirect free kick to the other side if play has had to be stopped.

Question
(Answer on page 98.)

Question 13 A player is standing 5 yards behind a colleague when the ball comes in his direction. Seeing his colleague move to intercept the ball, he shouts 'Leave it!' There are no opponents close to play. What action should the referee take?

This problem is more frequently found among less experienced players. The referee should advise players to use their name, so that they shout 'John Smith's ball!' or 'Goalkeeper's ball!' to avoid confusion.

(ii) Climbing on the back of a colleague
From time to time a player will climb on the back of a colleague in order to gain height when heading the ball. This is 'ungentlemanly' and gives an unfair advantage to his side. The referee should award an indirect free kick to the other side when this occurs, and caution the offending player.

(iii) Impeding the goalkeeper when the ball is being kicked into play
Occasionally a player will try to obstruct or distract the goalkeeper when he is putting the ball into play by jumping in front of him or gesticulating in some way. Again, this should be penalised by an indirect free kick to the non-offending side.

(iv) Dissent
Sometimes a player will dissent from a refereeing decision with the ball still in play. The referee should stop the game in order to issue the caution, and should re-start with an indirect free kick to the opposition from where the offence occurred.

Part 4
Dealing with misconduct

A referee once wrote: 'If you can keep your head while those around are losing theirs and blaming it on you, you've just missed the most blatant foul in the whole game.'

'Keeping your head' is the most important skill the referee needs when dealing with misconduct by players. Mistakes made here may inflame an already difficult and tense situation, and the referee needs good man-management skills if he is to maintain a calm control and the continued respect of the players.

The most important advice here is to aim at *prevention* rather than *cure*. An unfair tackle early in the game, or a bit of 'needle' developing between two players, can often be nipped in the bud quickly by a quiet word

'If you can keep your head . . .' Whatever the circumstances, try to remain calm and in control

It is useful for the referee to have a quiet word with a player if necessary to let him know that he is aware of what the player is doing and is unhappy with it

of warning and a free kick. Failure to pick up such problems can result in unwanted escalation later in the game. A recent survey of misconduct by the Cornwall County FA showed that less experienced referees were more likely to caution or send off players than more experienced officials. There may be several reasons for this, but I am sure that inexperienced referees are less likely to spot the seeds of trouble in their early sages, and thus are forced to take more punitive action later.

Often, a quiet warning can have good effect. It shows the player that the referee is aware of what he has done and that he is not prepared to accept this behaviour. When speaking to a player, the referee should not lecture him in an arrogant or irritable way, but calmly let him know the position and warn him accordingly. I also believe that it is better to speak quietly and discretely to him, rather than bawling him out in front of others. If the referee can do so in the course of the game, so much the better.

Above all, he should never touch a player. This can cause considerable offence. The referee has no right to do this and it may encourage the player to touch the referee back a little more aggressively. The referee should be firm and fair, treating the player with respect, but not leaving him in any doubt as to what he is expected to do.

Finally, the referee should never make a threat that he might not carry out. He should never say 'I'm sending off the next player who swears' unless he really *does* intend to carry this out. If the referee fails to be true to his word, he will lose the respect of the players very quickly and become something of a joke.

Cautions and sendings-off

At some time, it becomes necessary to take a player's name and report him for misconduct, either by giving a caution or by sending him off. For less serious offences, a caution is given and the player's misdeeds are reported on a caution report form. A player can be cautioned under four headings, which are easily remembered by the acronym DUPE.

D *A player shall be cautioned if he shows by word or action DISSENT from any decision given by the referee.*

U *He is guilty of UNGENTLEMANLY CONDUCT.*

P *He PERSISTENTLY infringes the laws of the game.*

E *He ENTERS or re-enters the field of play to join or re-join his team after play has commenced, or leaves the field of play during the progress of the game (except through accident) without, in either case, first having received a signal from the referee showing him that he may do so.*

Dissent

Dissent from the referee's decision is often verbal, with the player simply complaining about a decision. Occasionally it takes the form of some action, such as petulantly kicking the ball away after a decision by the referee, or making a gesture such as waving the arms in disgust. When this happens, the referee should caution the player concerned.

Question

(Answer on page 98.)

Question 14 The referee awards a free kick. After the kick is taken and the ball is in play, a player complains to the referee about the decision. The referee decides to caution him for dissent but has to stop the game to do this. How is the game re-started?

A useful piece of advice here is for the referee to try to avoid trouble before it occurs. Once again, prevention is better than cure. Often you will notice how the referee in a professional game will run to the centre circle after a goal is scored *before* recording the goal in his notebook. This does not guarantee that players will not commit dissent, but they will have to run to the centre circle to do so. Players often do foolish things in the heat of the moment, but calm down very quickly. Staying in the penalty area might invite a player to make a comment which might be avoided if the referee has gone some distance away.

Ungentlemanly conduct

This is by far the most common reason for cautioning a player since this heading, meaning *conduct unbecoming of a gentleman*, covers every type of minor villainy. A deliberate and hard foul tackle, cheating in some form, holding a player and many other offences, are punished by a caution under this heading. This does not mean that the referee must *always* caution a player who commits one of these offences. He must make a decision based on the severity of the offence. A hard two-footed tackle, for example, aimed at an opponent, should result normally in a caution, while a late tackle in which the opponent narrowly got to the ball before the offending player, might not. Remember, however, that there is a limit to the number of 'quiet words' the referee can reasonably have with a player before cautioning him.

Right *The referee should not allow a player to change his mind when a caution is necessary*

Question
(Answer on page 98.)

Question 15   A player deliberately grabs an opponent's shirt, but the referee allows the advantage. Play continues for a further 3 minutes before the ball goes out of play. Can the referee now caution the offending player?

Persistently infringing the laws

The use of this heading for a caution applies to when a player commits a string of minor but irritating offences, each of which is individually too minor to merit a caution for ungentlemanly conduct. An example of this would be a player encroaching by 2 yards at a corner kick, causing the kick to be re-taken, and then deliberately obstructing an opponent who has passed him with the ball, while a few minutes later holding on to the ball to delay the opposition's attempt to take a quick free kick. Each offence, in itself, is minor, but when taken together the player is unfairly distracting the opposition.

Entering or re-entering the field of play without permission

It is quite rare that a player will intentionally enter or re-enter the field without permission. If one does, however, he should be cautioned.

Question
(Answer on page 98.)

Question 16   The referee stops the game to caution a player for entering the field without permission. How should the game be re-started?

Occasionally a team will forget to tell the referee that a substitution has been made at half-time. When this occurs, the referee should caution the player concerned. Once again, prevention rather than cure is the order of the day, so he should remember to ask each side if they have any substitutes on before the second half commences.

Finally, it is a good idea to count the players before the start of the game. This is partly to make sure that each team does not have *more* than 11 players, and partly to see if they have *less* than 11. Of course, the team *can* start with less than 11 players, and if this is so the additional players can join at any time. If the referee is aware of this fact, he can simply wave on the late-arriving player as soon as he requests it. Failure to count the players before the start will lead to confusion in the referee's mind as he will wonder why further players wish to join the side.

Left 'But I went for the ball ref!' The referee should not let players talk him out of taking the right course of action

Sending off offences

Players can be sent off for offences under four headings.

(1) Serious foul play.
(2) Violent conduct.
(3) Foul or abusive language.
(4) Commiting a second cautionable offence.

When this happens, the offending players leave the field and are forbidden to take any further part in the game.

Questions
(Answers on page 98.)

Question 17 If during a game a referee cautions a player and at the conclusion of the match the player sincerely apologises, should the referee decide not to submit the report?

Question 18 With the ball in play, a player punches a colleague who retaliates by head-butting him. The referee stops the game and sends both players off. How does the referee re-start the game?

Incidents involving violence are usually the most explosive, and may require swift and decisive action by the referee. The offending players should be dealt with quickly and efficiently. If two players have been involved in a fight, and they are both being sent off, the referee should try to ensure that they return to the dressing room by different routes, or perhaps with a delay between them to stop the fight from re-commencing once they have left the field of play. Included under this heading is the offence of spitting. Any player seen committing this offence should be sent off for violent conduct.

Serious foul play

A referee must distinguish between what he considers to be 'foul play' and '*serious* foul play'. There is no clearly defined dividing line between these two terms, and it is a matter for the referee's judgment as to how to interpret them. Broadly speaking, serious foul play occurs when a player commits a physical act of excessive force or violence, committed with the clear intention of hurting an opponent or stopping him from either completing a skilful move or scoring a goal. Offences here may thus include the 'over-the-top tackle' in which an opponent raises his foot over the ball in a tackle, and thus digs his studs into the other player's leg. Another example would be a rugby tackle on an opponent, or where a player is charged violently, or has his hair pulled. In recent years, the meaning of the term 'serious foul play' has been broadened to include a foul tackle aimed at robbing an opponent of a clear goalscoring opportunity. This includes a situation in which a player deliberately trips or pushes an opponent, but also when a player deliberately handles the ball to stop it entering the goal or reaching an opponent who is placed in a strong position to score.

Violent conduct

Violent conduct refers to violent acts which occur outside the action of the game itself, or which are taken against officials, spectators or colleagues. This may happen when a player simply assaults someone else, but also includes such things as obscene gestures, indecent exposure and spitting at another person.

Persisting in misconduct after having received a caution

Once a player has received a caution, the committing of a second cautionable offence should be punished by the player being sent off. This can occur when, for example, a player commits dissent and is then guilty of ungentlemanly conduct. In this case the referee should submit a separate report for each offence when reporting the player.

Using foul or abusive language

The laws require the referee to send off players who use foul or abusive language. This does not necessarily have to be directed at the referee. It needs to be quoted on the report. The language can be foul, simply crude or obscene, or alternatively abusive, which does not have to be obscene.

Cautioning or sending off a player

Similarly to when the referee is having a quiet word with a player, some tact and diplomacy is needed here. The player is likely to be agitated or upset, so if the referee really wants to make him more volatile, he will find it very easy to do so. It is important to be clear and firm, and not to show anger or irritation.

If the referee wishes to take a player's name, and the player has moved some distance away, there is a temptation to blow the whistle and order the player over. This could well enrage him and, in any case, can be very embarrassing for the referee if he refuses to come. On the other hand, it is not a good idea to chase the player across the field and end up facing him completely out of breath. It is best to try to meet the player half-way. The referee should ask him to come over, and then walk towards him without rushing.

When the referee meets the player, he must ask for his full name and explain to him that he is being cautioned or sent off. It is not necessary to give every detail of why he is being cautioned, but just the heading. Experienced referees often tell a player that he is being cautioned before asking his name. But don't tell a player he is being sent off until you have noted it down.

It is important to get his *full* name. Sometimes a player will refuse to give his name, or even give an obviously false name. If a player refuses to give his name, it is a good idea to ask him to take a deep breath and try to remember. Often, players calm down after a few seconds and will then give their name. If they continue to refuse to do so, it is possible to send the report in with no name. This is very unusual, and players and their clubs generally realise that the governing body will pursue them to discover the name of the offending player. As a result, any fines imposed will be higher.

If a player gives an absurd name, the referee should ask him to reconsider.

Using red and yellow cards

To make clear his decision to spectators and to players and club officials, it is necessary that the referee shows a yellow card when cautioning a player and a red one when sending a player off. The card should be held high with the arm vertical, after the player's name has been taken. When a player is being sent off following a second cautionable offence, the referee should first show a yellow card, and then a red card, to make it clear that the player has committed a second cautionable offence, rather than a sending off offence.

Question
(Answer on page 98.)

Question 19   A player commits an act of misconduct during the half-time interval. Can the referee take action?

Misconduct by club officials and spectators

From time to time, the referee has to deal with club officials who are abusive or threatening, or who otherwise misbehave. If the referee feels that action beyond a verbal warning is required, then he should take the name of the person concerned and report the misbehaviour accordingly. I have only had to send in a report on a manager on one occasion, when the gentleman concerned had not kept fully up to date with the changes in the law on the goalkeeper's possession of the ball. After remonstrating with me and ignoring my warnings, he continued to argue and became abusive, so I had little alternative but to ask for his name. If it is possible

When cautioning a player, the referee should remain firm and in control, but he should always remember to treat players with respect

When the referee has made his decision to take action against a player, he should keep his resolve

to warn the official then do so. Sometimes, removing the official from the dug-out and into the stand may solve the problem.

A club is responsible for its spectators. If they are unruly or violent, then this too can be reported and the club will be asked to account for the incident. This is difficult when a game is being played on a local park where anyone can come and go. Where a club charges admission, however, the situation is very different. The club has a duty to take whatever action it can to ensure good behaviour by its supporters.

Filling in the report

Perhaps the most unpopular and arduous task faced by the referee is that of completing a misconduct report form. In fact, this is so arduous a task that some referees fail to send them in at all! This is a serious omission and much frowned upon by the authorities, and for good reason. If referees fail to send in reports, this makes things more difficult for subsequent referees at that team's games. The assumption is that other referees will have a double standard here, and will also be prepared to overlook cautions. It can rebound very badly on a referee when reports are not handed in.

A colleague once sent a player off and failed to submit a report, an action which led to his career eventually collapsing. Normally, a copy of the report is sent by the County FA to the club concerned, for its information and any relevant comments. When the club had heard nothing, it wrote and asked if, perhaps, the report had been lost in the post, and if another copy could be sent. Of course, the FA had no record of the incident and thus wrote to the referee for his observations. The FA then suspended him and, ultimately, his once promising career was finished, and he was dropped from the senior league in which he was then refereeing.

While filling in misconduct reports can be time-consuming and awkward, it is essential that the referee spends some time and effort on this chore. At best, mistakes are embarrassing and humiliating; at worst, players may appeal successfully if errors are apparent in the report. Referees are encouraged to follow a simple procedure.

(1) Quote the *full* name of the player and his club, and use first names. There may be more than one J. Smith in a team, so the use of a player's full name is necessary to avoid confusion.
(2) The offence for which the player is being cautioned or sent off must be clearly stated. This is made easier by the layout of the form, and simply requires the referee to fill in a letter in the appropirate box.
(3) Clearly but briefly state what happened. The report does not require a deep discussion of the game or other incidents within it, but simply a description of the offence for which the player is being reported. The referee should try to be both precise and concise in this.

(4) The referee should state the *time* that the incident occurred, *where* it occurred, and his own position at the time.

(5) Reports must be submitted in duplicate, with a third copy retained by the referee for reference. This is important if there is an appeal by the player which results in a personal hearing to which the referee will be expected to come to answer questions about his actions.

(6) It is important to check spelling and grammar in the report. The best advice here is to write the report out in rough to start with, before entering it on to the report form. Mistakes here make the referee look foolish when the report is received by the club.

(7) Every separate incident needs a separate report. This means that if the referee has cautioned a player early in the game, and sent him off later, the referee must write *two* reports, one for each incident.

(8) The report must be submitted within two working days. Good advice here is to use a first class stamp!

If the referee is still confused when he comes to complete his first misconduct form, I advise him to contact someone with experience, to check it over and help him re-write it if necessary.

Assaults on the referee

Although assaults on referees have become a disturbingly more common problem, they are still, mercifully, rare. Looking at the number of assaults in a recent season, I calculated that statistically a referee is likely to be assaulted only once every 40 seasons. The problem is that when it does occur, the referee may be taken by surprise and thus not ready to deal with it. If it happens, the referee should follow some simple guidelines.

(1) **Decide whether or not to abandon the game.** In the case of serious injury, this may be a very straightforward decision. Often, however, referees try to carry on and then realise that they are concussed, suffering from double vision, or just very shaken up. If in *any* doubt, the referee is advised to abandon the game, especially if he needs medical attention.

(2) **Obtain names and addresses of witnesses.** This may not always be practicable, but if at all possible the referee should do so because it makes any subsequent civil or criminal action much simpler.

(3) **Notify the police if actual bodily harm has been done.** It is important that the referee does this as quickly as possible so that the police can interview the parties and talk to witnesses.

(4) **Report the whole matter to the appropriate authority.** The referee is advised to do this both in writing and by telephone. Normally the player concerned will be suspended immediately, and the secretary of the authority will need to be informed quickly so that he can do this.

(5) **Inform the Referees' Association local secretary.** Most referees join the Referees' Association, and thus gain the advantage of legal advice and support. Injury suffered and time lost from work may require the referee to sue the player concerned in civil court, and the RA will help here.

(6) **Keep a copy of all correspondence.**

(7) **Inform the appropriate authority and RA secretary of the result of any prosecution.**

Naturally, with the incidence of assault still low, most referees may officiate for many years without being affected. Assault, however, may be totally unexpected. One referee suffered a serious assault after asking a spectator to move his young son back a few paces from the line as he was concerned for the small boy's safety. A few years ago, two referees in the city where I lived suffered serious assaults in pre-season 'friendlies'. Forewarned is forearmed!

Answers

Question 1   The referee should award a penalty kick. A penalty is awarded according to where the *incident* occurred and not where the *ball* was when it happened.

Question 2   Stop play. Both players should be sent off for violent conduct. The game should be re-started with a dropped ball from where the ball was when the referee stopped the game. A penalty should not be awarded because the incident occurred off the field of play (i.e. behind the goal line).

Question 3   This is deliberate handball and the referee should award a penalty. Since the player has unfairly stopped an almost certain goal, the law now requires that he should be sent off for serious foul play. If the goal is scored, the player should be cautioned.

Question 4   No action. The position of the goalkeeper's hands are important here, and provided he handles the ball within the area, he has done nothing wrong.

Question 5   This represents handball, and the referee should award a direct free kick to the opponents, to be taken from where the ball was handled.

Question 6   No action. The referee should not penalise *unintentional* handball.

Question 7   No. If the referee considers that the behaviour of the player merits a caution, then he should not hesitate to take action.

Question 8   The referee should give an indirect free kick *against* the player trying to head the ball. By putting himself in a dangerous position, the player is unfairly distracting the opponent.

Question 9 No action. Provided the defender who headed the ball has not done so in a deliberate effort to circumvent the laws (by heading it on after it has been deliberately chipped up in the air by a colleague, for example).

Question 10 (a) If the goalkeeper picks the ball up, he should be penalised by the award of an indirect free kick from where the offence occurred. If the offence occurred within the goal area, the free kick should be taken from the nearest point on the edge of the 6-yard area parallel to the goal line. (b) No action.

Question 11 The goalkeeper can do this for as long as he likes. It is only when he takes control of the ball in his hands that he may be accused of time wasting. The referee should point this out to the opponent who is complaining.

Question 12 The referee should stop the game. Although the player is off the field of play, he should still be dealt with and reported by the referee for violent conduct. The game should be re-started with an indirect free kick from where the ball was when play was stopped.

Question 13 No action. The player does not gain an unfair advantage and should not be penalised.

Question 14 The game is re-started by awarding an indirect free kick to the opposition, to be taken from the place where the offence occurred.

Question 15 Yes. Although the referee has allowed the advantage, he may take action later.

Question 16 By an indirect free kick to the player's opponents to be taken from where the ball was when the offence occurred.

Question 17 No. All cautions or sendings-off *must* be reported to the authority under which the game is being played.

Question 18 The game should be re-started by an indirect free kick to the opponents, to be taken from where the offence occurred.

Question 19 Yes. The referee *can* take action during the half-time interval.

Unit 5
Free kicks and penalty kicks

Part 1
Free kicks

During the game the referee will award two types of free kick: direct and indirect. To remind yourself of what we considered in Unit 4, check back on:

(a) the nine penal offences for which a direct free kick can be awarded
(b) the five offences for which an indirect free kick is awarded.

The difference between a direct and an indirect free kick is that it is possible to score a goal 'directly' against the opposing team from a direct free kick without the ball being touched by another player. If the ball is kicked directly into goal from an indirect free kick, the referee should award a goal kick, or a corner kick if it is kicked by a player into his own goal.

To ensure that players are aware that the referee has given an indirect free kick, he is required to keep his arm vertically upright at the taking of the kick. Quite frequently players will ask whether a kick is direct or indirect, even when the referee has punished an obvious penal offence such as deliberate handball or a trip. If the kick is near to goal, and awarded to the attacking side, a useful piece of advice is to *always* tell the goalkeeper if it is direct or indirect. This is not required by the laws, but it helps to avoid misunderstandings and subsequent argument, and thus prevents problems occurring when a goal is disputed or claimed.

Refer to the laws and now answer the following questions.

Questions
(Answers on page 114.)

Question 1 How long should the referee keep his arm vertical at the taking of an indirect free kick?

Question 2 An indirect free kick is awarded. The ball is kicked directly into the opponent's goal. Unfortunately, the referee has failed to raise his arm indicating that the kick is indirect. The scoring team protests because the referee refuses to allow the goal. Is the referee correct in his decision?

Question 3   Can a free kick be passed backwards?

The conditions for a correctly taken free kick

The laws require certain conditions to be met for a free kick to be correctly taken.

(A) The ball must be stationary

A team could gain an unfair advantage if a player was allowed to kick a moving ball at a free kick, since it may be possible to kick it further. Also, because the opposition is expecting the ball to be 'dead' before being kicked, there is likely to be some confusion and it would be unjust to allow the game to continue if this occurs.

Question
(Answer on page 114.)

Question 4   What should the referee do if a free kick is taken when the ball is not stationary? How should he re-start the game?

(B) The kick must take place from where the incident occurred

This is, of course, simple common sense. An exception is made, however, if the incident occurred within one team's goal area. If the kick is an indirect one to the attacking side, then it should be taken from the nearest point on the 6-yard line. If it is a direct or an indirect kick to the defending side, it can be taken from anywhere within the goal area. It is also simple common sense to remember that the referee cannot always be sure *exactly* where every incident occurred. If the free kick is near to the half-way line, then it is less important for it to be taken in the precise place where the offence occurred than if it was just outside the penalty area and awarded to the attacking side. It is wise to be more strict with this when the ball is nearer to the goal.

(C) Opposing players must be at least 10 yards from the ball

Opposing players gain a considerable advantage by standing less than 10 yards from the ball or, as the laws phrase it, 'encroaching'. Often, when the attacking side is awarded a kick in these circumstances, the referee will have problems in ensuring that they retreat the full distance and that, having done so, they remain there until the ball is played.

If players encroach they may be cautioned, and this is sometimes used as a last resort by the referee to ensure that the side taking the free kick is not disadvantaged, and the re-start of the game delayed.

You may decide to pace out 10 yards and then insist that the players, frequently lined up in a 'wall', retreat the full distance. The danger with this approach is that when your back is turned, the attacking side may push the ball forwards a couple of yards. It is not recommended for the referee to turn his back on the ball unless he has a neutral linesman who can keep an eye on this for him. Far better to stand over the ball and gesture to the players to move back until satisfied that they are 10 yards from the ball.

Players often want to take a quick free kick. If this is the case, then the referee should allow this to happen. Attackers will want to get the game moving quickly, and thus seek a quick free kick while the defence is still disorganised and confused. Remember that defenders may not have had a chance to retreat the full 10 yards. If the ball hits a defender in these circumstances, the referee should allow play to continue because this is a risk which the attacking side has opted to take.

With a free kick to the attacking side just outside the defending penalty area, both sides will wish to take up appropriate positions. When he is happy that the defending side is at least 10 yards from the ball and everyone is ready, the referee will want to be in a suitable position. Free kicks such as this are known as 'ceremonial free kicks', and the referee should give a good, clear indication that the game can re-start by blowing his whistle hard and clear.

Questions
(Answers on page 114.)

Question 5   The referee has awarded a free kick to the attacking team just 5 yards from the edge of the defending team's penalty area. A defender stands 5 yards *behind* the ball. Is he allowed to do this?

Question 6   A free kick is awarded for a foul just 4 or 5 yards from the touch line. A player wishes to take a quick free kick. The referee signals his approval and the kick is taken. Unfortunately, the player miskicks the ball over the touch line. He appeals for the kick to be re-taken because an opponent was only 2 or 3 yards from the ball. The kicker alleges that he was 'put off' by the close proximity of the opponent. What should be the referee's decision?

(D) The referee must signal for the re-start of play

As stated above, the referee should give a clear signal, preferably a blast on his whistle, when re-starting at a ceremonial free kick. If the game has been stopped due to injury, again it is a good idea to re-start with a clear whistle so that there are no misunderstandings about what is happening.

If the free kick is to be taken in the middle of the field of play, or if the

team wishes to take a quick free kick, then the use of the whistle may not be necessary. In fact, over-use of the whistle may be distracting and may reduce its impact when it is *really* needed. A signal may not be needed at all; at other times the referee simply needs to shout 'Play on!' to ensure that the game keeps moving smoothly.

(E) The ball must travel its own circumference

You will already know that the ball's circumference is 27–28 inches, and the ball must travel this distance before it is in play. If it does not, order the kick to be re-taken.

Questions
(Answers on pages 114–15.)

Question 7   At a free kick, the ball does not travel its full circumference before one player strikes another. The referee stops the game and sends the offending player off. How should the game be re-started?

Question 8   A free kick is taken and the player taking it touches it a second time before the ball has touched another player. What action should the referee take?

(F) The ball must be touched by another player before the kicker touches it a second time

Once the ball is in play – that is, when it has travelled its own circumference – the player taking the kick will be penalised if he touches it before another player makes contact with it. If this occurs, the referee should award an indirect free kick to be taken from where the player made contact with the ball for a second time.

Question
(Answer on page 115.)

Question 9   A free kick is awarded. The ball rebounds from the referee, whereupon the player who took the kick plays it for a second time. What action, if any, should the referee take?

Free kicks in the penalty area to the defending side

A free kick may be given inside the penalty area to the defending side. If this happens, there are several conditions which must be adhered to.

Left It is not necessary for the referee to blow the whistle for every re-start of play, but sometimes it is important to use the whistle to show that he means business

(A) The ball has to leave the penalty area before it is in play

If play is stopped due to an infringement *before* the ball has left the penalty area, but after the ball has been kicked, the game must re-start with the original free kick, because the ball is not in play until it has left the area.

(B) Attacking players must be at least 10 yards from the ball at the taking of the kick, and remain outside the penalty area until the ball is in play

If an attacker 'encroaches' by entering the penalty area before the ball has left it, the kick should be re-taken. Of course, if the defending side is able to move the ball forwards, and would gain no advantage from a free kick, the referee can apply the advantage clause and simply play on.

(C) If the offence occurs within the goal area, the ball may be placed anywhere in the goal area where the offence occurred

The defender can select the best position in the goal area and take the kick from that point.

Free kicks in the penalty area to the attacking side

If one of the nine penal offences is committed by a defending player against an opponent within the penalty area when the ball is in play, the referee must award a penalty. For one of the non-penal offences, the referee must award an indirect free kick from the place where the incident occurred. When this occurs, certain conditions apply.

(A) The defenders must be at least 10 yards from the ball, or on the goal line and between the goal posts

If the attacking side has an indirect free kick 8 yards from the goal line, the defenders can stand less than 10 yards from the ball so long as they stand on the goal line between the posts. They cannot stand on the goal line outside the posts, if this is closer than 10 yards.

(B) If the offence occurred within the goal area, the free kick should be taken from the nearest point on the 6-yard line

This change in the law was introduced a few years ago to avoid the problems created for referees when a kick had to be awarded very close to, or on, the goal line. Remember, the defending players may still stand on the goal line, so long as they are between the posts.

Questions
(Answers on page 115.)

Question 10   At a free kick near the goal, to be taken by the attacking side, the goalkeeper protests to the referee that an opponent is standing on the goal line next to him. May the referee take any action?

Question 11   A free kick is awarded to the defending side within its own penalty area. The ball is mishit and goes over the goal line – but not into the goal – before it has left the penalty area. What is the referee's decision?

Free kicks struck into a player's own goal

Often a player will hit a free kick back to his own goalkeeper. Very occasionally, the ball may be kicked too hard, or the goalkeeper may be inattentive or he may slip, with the result that the ball goes into the goal. If this happens, the referee must award a corner kick because the laws state that a goal cannot be scored directly into a player's own goal from a free kick of any description.

Question
(Answer on page 115.)

Question 12   A defender takes a free kick just outside his own penalty area, and plays the ball back towards the goalkeeper. Unfortunately, he has not noticed that the goalkeeper is lying injured. Realising that the ball is going into the net, the defender chases after it. Just before the ball can enter the goal, the defender reaches it but slices his kick so that the ball goes over the line into the goal. What action should the referee take?

Part 2 _____
Penalty kicks

If a defending player commits one of the nine penal offences within the penalty area, when the ball is in play, the attacking side should be awarded a penalty.

Question
(Answer on page 115.)

Question 13 Which one penal offence is not committed against an opponent?

The award of a penalty is often a critical point in a match. Players normally score from such a kick. In a tight game, the referee's decision here is absolutely critical. Perhaps the worst of any referee's memories concern penalties he should have given but did not, and those he gave but should not have. What at first glance appears a straightforward law is actually rather complicated, but I will take it stage by stage.

The position of players at a penalty kick
Outfield players

The law requires that, with the exception of the penalty taker and the goalkeeper, all players should be positioned:

(a) at least 10 yards from the ball
(b) outside the penalty area
(c) on the field of play.

To ensure that players are at least 10 yards from the ball, an arc is drawn 10 yards from the penalty spot, and all players should be outside this arc.

At first it seems odd to insist that players remain on the field of play, but this makes more sense if you consider what an unscrupulous player might do to distract either the goalkeeper or the kicker if he were allowed to walk off before the penalty was taken.

The law demands that the kicker is identified *before* the kick is taken. This fairly recent change in the law has been introduced to avoid the 'gamesmanship' which occurred in the past when one player carefully put the ball on the spot, turned his back on it to walk away a few steps and, once outside the area, was passed by another forward running in at high speed to take the penalty. Once the referee is clear as to who is taking the

penalty, he should tell the goalkeeper so that it is clear to him who he will
be facing when the whistle is blown for the kick to be taken.

No other player is allowed to enter the penalty area until the ball has
been struck. If players do enter or 'encroach' into the penalty area, there
are a number of actions the referee must take.

Questions

(Answers on page 115.)

Question 14 At the taking of a penalty kick, a defender encroaches, and a goal is not scored. What action should the referee take?

Question 15 At the taking of a penalty, an attacker encroaches before the ball is struck, and a goal is scored. What action should the referee take?

We can draw up a simple chart to show what the referee should do if offences occur at the taking of the penalty.

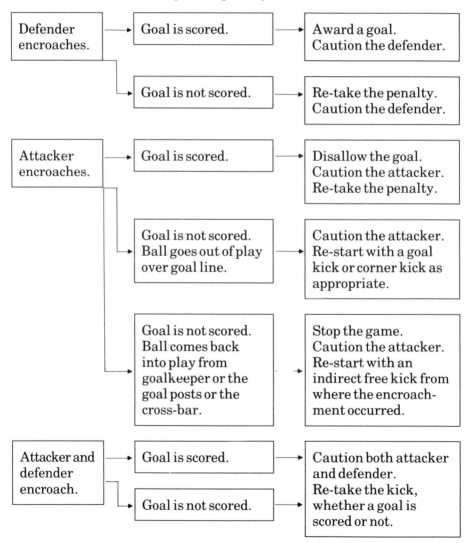

Defender encroaches.	Goal is scored.	Award a goal. Caution the defender.
	Goal is not scored.	Re-take the penalty. Caution the defender.
Attacker encroaches.	Goal is scored.	Disallow the goal. Caution the attacker. Re-take the penalty.
	Goal is not scored. Ball goes out of play over goal line.	Caution the attacker. Re-start with a goal kick or corner kick as appropriate.
	Goal is not scored. Ball comes back into play from goalkeeper or the goal posts or the cross-bar.	Stop the game. Caution the attacker. Re-start with an indirect free kick from where the encroachment occurred.
Attacker and defender encroach.	Goal is scored.	Caution both attacker and defender. Re-take the kick, whether a goal is scored or not.
	Goal is not scored.	

The goalkeeper

At the taking of the penalty kick, the goalkeeper must stand:

(a) on his goal line
(b) between the goal posts.

He must not move his feet until the ball has been kicked.

Question
(Answer on page 115.)

Question 16 If the goalkeeper moves his feet before the penalty kick has been taken, but after the referee has blown his whistle, what action should the referee take?

A simple chart can help to explain the referee's actions in this case.

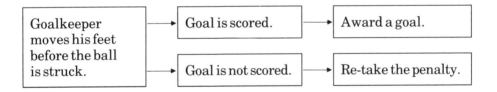

In neither case is it necessary to caution the goalkeeper. Another offence which can occur here is the penalty taker checking his run, encouraging the goalkeeper to move before the ball is struck. Where this happens the kick should be re-taken if a goal is scored, because this behaviour is seen as unfair.

Questions
(Answers on page 115.)

Question 17 Must the ball be played forwards at a penalty?

Question 18 A penalty kick is awarded. The ground is extremely muddy and slippery. As the kicker runs forwards, he slips and moves the ball forwards about a yard. One of his team-mates then runs in from outside the area from an onside position and scores. Should the referee award the goal?

Question 19 The player taking a penalty mishits the ball and only manages to kick it a yard or so. He then touches the ball a second time. What action should the referee take?

Outside agents

Very occasionally, an 'outside agent' will come into contact with the ball. An outside agent is any person or thing which intrudes on to the field of play, including spectators, dogs, overhead wires or even a ball coming on from an adjacent game.

(a) If the ball comes into contact with an outside agent on its way towards the goal, re-take the penalty.
(b) If this happens when the ball rebounds into play from the goalkeeper, or the posts, or the cross-bar, re-start play with a dropped ball from the place where the contact with the outside agent occurred.

Of course, neither of these occurrences is very common, but if and when they do occur, it is important to be alert to the action you must take. In particular, remember that you do *not* re-take the penalty if the ball hits the outside agent after rebounding into play.

A penalty kick in extended time

If a penalty kick is awarded close to the end of a half, the referee is instructed to *extend* time for the penalty to be taken. Very simply, this means that once the referee has decided whether a goal has been scored, the half is over. Only the kicker and the goalkeeper are involved. Once the outcome of the kick has been resolved, the half is over.

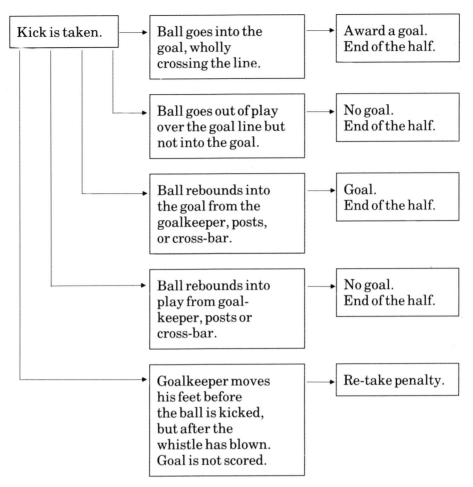

My advice here is that if the referee awards a penalty kick and extends the time for it to be taken, he should inform all the players of what is happening. This avoids the difficulty of explaining why he is not awarding a goal when the ball is struck in from the rebound, or from a further penalty if an offence is committed by a defender immediately following the kick. This makes his job considerably easier.

The position of the referee and linesman at a penalty kick

You will now appreciate that the referee and linesman have a great deal to look out for at a penalty kick. Referees have different ideas as to the best position for officials.

One common position was shown in Unit 1, and is reproduced below. Here the linesman is positioned to act as a 'goal judge', signalling if a goal is scored, and sometimes checking the goalkeeper's movement. The referee judges encroachment and sometimes movement by the goalkeeper.

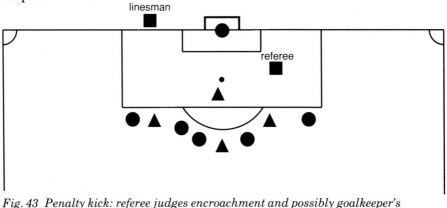

Fig. 43 Penalty kick: referee judges encroachment and possibly goalkeeper's movement; linesman acts as 'goal judge'

The problem with this position is that it is difficult for the referee to judge encroachment in addition to keeping an eye on the goalkeeper, especially if he is looking for the goalkeeper's movement as well.

An alternative is shown below. Here the linesman is brought on to the field of play to check for encroachment, which is the most difficult offence to see clearly. He can also see if there is any jostling or other misdemeanour occurring amongst the players. Meanwhile, the referee is looking at the player taking the kick and the goalkeeper, to make sure that they comply with the law.

This method is only feasible if you have a neutral linesman. It suffers

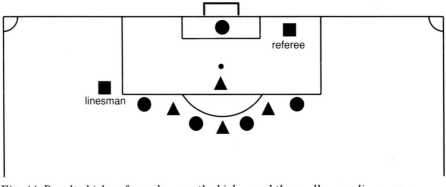

Fig. 44 Penalty kick: referee observes the kicker and the goalkeeper; linesman checks for encroachment

from the disadvantage that if the ball rebounds from the post or the goal-keeper, the linesman may have difficulty in regaining his position quickly. However, it is used by a number of referees.

Question
(Answer on page 115.)

Question 20 A team is awarded a penalty kick during a game. The usual penalty taker is a substitute. May a player of that team be withdrawn and the substitute allowed to go on and take the kick?

Deciding the result of a game by kicks from the penalty mark

It is possible for matches to be decided on kicks from the penalty mark at the end of extra time if the game is still drawn. The law is now well described in the *Referee's Chart* with a check list to make understanding easier. The diagram below shows the positions to be taken up by players and officials.

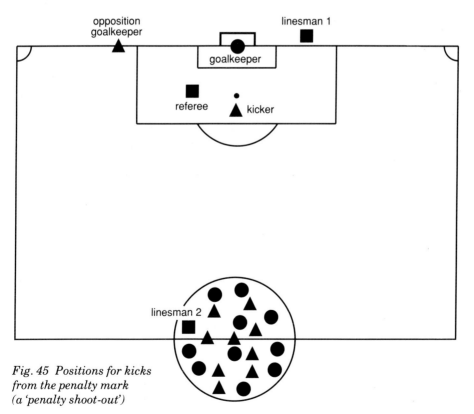

Fig. 45 Positions for kicks from the penalty mark (a 'penalty shoot-out')

Questions

(Answers on pages 115–16.)

Question 21 Which team takes the first kick at the taking of kicks from the penalty mark to decide the game?

Question 22 Which goal should be used for taking the kicks?

Question 23 Where must all the players be, apart from the two goalkeepers and the player taking the kick?

Question 24 What should the referee do if it becomes too dark to complete the kicks?

Question 25 Under what circumstances might a substitute be used when the teams are taking kicks from the penalty mark to decide the result of the game?

Question 26 What is the role of the linesman at the taking of kicks from the penalty mark at the end of a game?

   Matches which are decided on kicks from the penalty mark are, mercifully, rare. However, they do pose a problem for the referee because with the law being rather complicated, the danger is that he referees the game with only a hazy recollection of the details involved. Since the result is at stake, it is important that he gets the details absolutely right. Every time I referee a match which could end in this way, I read and re-read the procedure beforehand to make absolutely certain that problems will not arise. I would urge others to do the same.

Answers

Question 1 The referee should keep his arm in the vertical position until the ball either goes out of play or is played by another player.

Question 2 Yes. The referee *should* have raised his arm, but cannot allow a goal from an indirect free kick.

Question 3 Yes. Only a penalty kick *must* be kicked forwards.

Question 4 Stop play. The referee should re-start play with the free kick, this time correctly taken.

Question 5 No. Opponents must be at least 10 yards from the ball in *any* direction.

Question 6 Award a throw-in to the other side. If a player takes a quick free kick, he must accept that he runs a risk of the ball hitting an opponent or of being put off.

Question 7 Since the ball had not gone the distance of its full circumference, it was not in play at the time of the offence. The game should therefore be re-started with the original free kick.

Question 8   Provided the ball has travelled its own circumference, the opposing side should be awarded an indirect free kick from where the player made contact with the ball for a second time. If the ball has not travelled its own circumference, the kick should be re-taken because the ball was not in play when it was kicked for a second time.

Question 9   So long as the ball has travelled its own circumference, an indirect free kick should be awarded to the opposing side. Although the ball has hit the referee before being touched a second time by the original player, the referee is seen as 'part of the field of play', and this does not count as making contact.

Question 10   The attacker is perfectly entitled to stand on the goal line next to the goalkeeper, so long as he does not obstruct or impede him.

Question 11   Re-take the free kick. The ball is not in play until the ball has left the penalty area.

Question 12   The correct decision is to award an indirect free kick to the attacking side from where the defender touched the ball for a second time.

Question 13   Deliberate handball (except, of course, by the goalkeeper in his own penalty area).

Question 14   Re-take the penalty. The law states that the defender should be cautioned.

Question 15   Re-take the penalty. Again, the offending player should be cautioned.

Question 16   The referee should take no action. If a goal is *not* scored, the kick must be re-taken. There is no stipulation that the goalkeeper be cautioned.

Question 17   Yes.

Question 18   Yes. This is quite acceptable, so long as the player who scores enters the area *after* the ball has been kicked.

Question 19   Stop play. Re-start with an indirect free kick to defending side.

Question 20   Yes. A substitution may be made at any time in the game.

Question 21   The team which has won the toss. Note that its captain does *not* have a choice.

Question 22   The referee decides which goal to use. In a junior game it may be wise to use the end nearer the changing rooms. Other factors such as the condition of the playing surface or the position of the spectators might influence the referee's decision.

Question 23 All the players, apart from the goalkeepers and the penalty taker, should be in the centre circle. If the referee is fortunate enough to have a neutral linesman, he should place one of them in the centre circle with the players to note the numbers of players taking kicks, and also to keep an eye on the players as they wait to take a penalty.

Question 24 The laws require the referee to decide the match by the drawing of lots or the toss of a coin.

Question 25 The only substitution allowed is for an injured goalkeeper.

Question 26 One linesman should act as a 'goal judge' and assist the referee at the taking of the kicks. The other linesman should remain in the centre circle with all the players (except the goalkeepers and the player taking a kick). This second linesman should note down the players going forwards to take a kick to ensure that no-one has a second kick before everyone else has had an attempt.

Unit 6
The throw-in, goal kick and corner kick

Part 1
The throw-in

If the ball passes completely over the touch line, the referee should award a throw-in to the opposite team to that of the player who last played it. There is a sequence of actions needed for a correctly taken throw-in to occur.

(1) The throw-in should be taken from the place where the ball left the field of play.
(2) Both of the player's feet must remain *on* or *behind* the touch line, as the ball is thrown.
(3) The ball should be thrown from behind and over the head.
(4) The ball should be *thrown* and not *dropped*.
(5) The ball must enter the field of play.
(6) The ball must be played by another player before it is played a second time by the player taking the throw.

From the list above it can be seen that the referee and the linesman on that touch line have a great deal to scrutinise. Any offence which results in the ball being incorrectly thrown in, is described as a 'foul throw'. It is penalised by the throw being awarded to the other side.

Questions
(Answers on page 125.)

Question 1 The player taking the throw-in advances 6 yards up the field from where the ball passed over the touch line before throwing it in. What is the referee's decision?

Question 2 The player taking the throw-in retreats 6 yards from where the ball passed over the touch line so that he can throw the ball back to his goalkeeper. What is the referee's decision?

The throw-in should be made from the place where the ball left the field of play

Players are loathe to lose the advantage gained from the throw-in by giving away a 'foul throw', with the result that they will often ask the referee where the throw should be taken from. The referee should always guide players to the correct place, and try to warn them first if they are about to throw the ball from the wrong position. Only give a foul throw for the ball being thrown in from the wrong place if the player has taken the throw too quickly for you to warn him. Generally, referees are unconcerned about players being a couple of yards out in the middle of the field. But if the throw-in is nearer to the goal, it is important to make sure that they do not gain an unfair advantage by advancing or retreating along the touch line.

Part of both of the player's feet shall remain on or behind the touch line when the throw is taken

It is important that the player's feet do not leave the ground as the throw is being taken. The reason for this is that the player can gain a considerable advantage by throwing the ball much further if he lifts his foot, and most players are aware of this. Often players misunderstand the part of the law which concerns the position of the feet. If the player's feet are as shown in the diagram below, the throw-in is perfectly legal – part of both feet are on or behind the line. However, remember that if the player lifts his toes off the ground as he throws the ball, it is a foul throw – he does not have part of both feet *on* or *behind* the line.

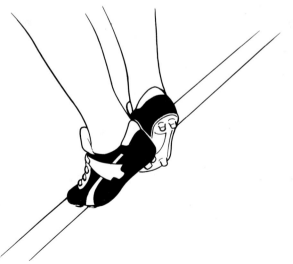

Fig. 46 Legal throw-in – part of both feet are on or behind the touch line

The ball shall be thrown from behind and over the head

The player should throw the ball with one hand on either side of the ball as shown below. The action of the throw should start *behind* the head, and the ball should be released after the ball has passed *over* the head.

The ball is sometimes thrown with a one-handed action, giving the thrower an unfair advantage because this puts more power into the throw. It is difficult to spot this, but the telltale sign is the fact that the ball spins in the air after it is thrown in this way.

Fig. 47 One hand must be on either side of the ball

The ball must be thrown and not dropped

A thrower may wish to throw the ball to a colleague only a short distance away. To do this, he may choose to drop the ball rather than throw it. This is not allowed, and is penalised by the throw being awarded to the opposition.

The ball enters the field of play

The ball must enter the field of play before it is in play at the taking of a throw-in.

Questions

(Answers on page 125.)

Question 3 At the taking of a throw-in, the ball fails to enter the field of play. What action should the referee take?

Question 4 A correctly taken throw-in is caught by the wind and blown out of play before it has been touched by another player. How does the referee re-start the game?

Question 5 A ball is thrown in correctly, but rolls along the touch line. What action should the referee take?

Question 6 A player takes a throw-in but kicks the ball before it has touched another player. What action should the referee take?

Question 7   A player taking a throw-in deliberately handles the ball in the field of play after it has been thrown in, but before it has been touched by another player. What action should the referee take?

When watching a throw-in, it is often the case that the referee and the linesman will look at different aspects of it. For example, the referee will instruct the linesman to look at the thrower's feet while he concentrates on the hands. Any fault observed by the linesman will lead him to signal clearly to the referee so that the throw-in can be awarded the other way.

The ball may be seen by the referee to clearly go out of play, but he may be unaware of who last touched it. A clear signal from the linesman is important here to indicate which side is entitled to the throw. There are times when the referee has clearly seen who last kicked the ball, but is unsure of whether it has wholly gone out of play. The linesman, being in a better position to judge this, can give a good signal to the referee to show him that a throw-in should be awarded.

It is important to try to maintain a clear understanding between the referee and his linesmen. Concentration and teamwork can ensure that errors are minimised.

Other aspects of the throw-in need to be considered . . .

Questions
(Answers on page 125.)

Question 8   Can a goalkeeper take a throw-in?

Question 9   When a throw-in is being taken, an opponent jumps up and down in front of the thrower. What action should the referee take?

Question 10   What should the referee do if the ball is thrown by a player directly into: (a) his opponents' goal; (b) his own goal?

Question 11   This is a situation which occurred to a colleague in a game recently, and which caused some argument among referees. A throw-in was awarded to the defending team about 15 yards from its goal line. A defender threw the ball back to his goalkeeper but failed to notice a forward, who ran quickly between him and the goalkeeper and intercepted the ball. The forward kicked the ball into the goal. The referee turned to see the linesman flag for a foul throw. What action should the referee take?

Part 2 _____
The goal kick

If the whole of the ball goes over the goal line, but does not enter the goal, having been last touched by an attacking player, the referee must award a goal kick. The procedure for a correctly taken goal kick is as follows.

The ball can be placed anywhere in the 6-yard area

In an effort to speed the game up, goal kicks may now be taken from anywhere in the goal area.

The ball must leave the penalty area before it is in play

This can be shown by considering the following questions.

Questions
(Answers on page 125.)

Question 12   A goal kick is taken. Before the ball has left the penalty area, the referee sees a player strike an opponent. What action should the referee take?

Question 13   A goal kick is accidentally kicked over the goal line before it has left the penalty area. What action should the referee take?

It is a valuable aid to the referee if the linesman observes carefully the taking of a goal kick to ensure that the ball leaves the area before it is touched by another player. If, for example, the ball comes to the edge of the area and is then passed back to the 'keeper by a defender before it has left the area, the referee should stop play and order the kick to be re-taken.

Attacking players must not enter the penalty area until the ball has passed out of it

Often a goalkeeper will take a short goal kick, passing the ball to a colleague just outside the penalty area. An attacker seeing this might run across the area to intercept the ball or challenge the defender. This is not allowed. The referee should insist that the kick is re-taken, and advise the attacker about this breach of the law.

There are two other aspects of the goal kick which you need to be aware of.

(1) A goal cannot be scored direct from a goal kick. If the ball directly

enters the opponents' goal from a goal kick, the referee should award a goal kick to the other side.

(2) A player cannot be offside if he receives the ball direct from a goal kick.

Many players, even at senior level, are unaware that it is impossible to be offside from a goal kick. This can result in some controversy if a goal is scored following such a move. A team I once played for used this as a tactic in the game. We had a strong centre-half who could kick the ball up-field into the opponent's half. Our centre-forward would stand about 15 yards 'offside', collect the ball and run for goal. Frequently, the opposition would besiege the referee demanding to know why offside had not been given. Meanwhile, my side would be waiting to re-start, one goal up.

Question

(Answer on page 125.)

Question 14   Apart from when the ball enters the opponents' goal direct from a goal kick, on what other occasions does the ball pass into the goal and a goal kick is awarded?

Part 3
The corner kick

If the ball passes over the goal line, but does not enter the goal, having been last touched by a defender, the referee must award a corner kick. A corner must be taken from inside the quadrant by the corner flag. When a corner is awarded, the following conditions must apply.

The ball must travel its own circumference

This is a standard condition for all re-starts of play which involve a kick. If the ball does not travel at least its own circumference, the kick must be re-taken.

Opponents must be positioned at least 10 yards from the ball

Until the ball is kicked, opponents must be at least 10 yards away. If they encroach, the referee should order the kick to be re-taken, unless there is no advantage to the attacking side in doing so.

The player taking the kick must not play the ball a second time until it has been touched by another player

Again, this is normal for any re-start of play at which the ball is kicked.

Question
(Answer on page 125.)

Question 15 The ball rebounds from the goal post at a corner to the player who originally took the kick, who touches it a second time. What action should the referee take?

It is worth remembering that it is impossible to be judged offside direct from a corner kick.

There is one other aspect of the corner kick to consider . . .

Question
(Answer on page 125.)

Question 16 Can a goal be scored direct from a corner kick?

Answers

Question 1   Foul throw. Award the throw-in to the other side, to be taken from where the ball left the field of play. Remember to advise the player about the correct place before he throws it, if this is practicable.

Question 2   Foul throw. The throw-in must be taken from where the ball left the field of play, and players cannot advance or retreat from this position.

Question 3   Re-take the throw. The ball is not in play until it has entered the field of play.

Question 4   Award a throw-in to the other side, to be taken from where the ball left the field of play following the throw-in.

Question 5   Play on. The markings are part of the field of play following the throw-in.

Question 6   Award an indirect free kick to the opposition to be taken from where the player kicked the ball. The ball must not be played by the thrower until it has been touched by another player.

Question 7   Award a direct free kick. The ball has been handled deliberately.

Question 8   Yes. There is no reason why the goalkeeper cannot take a throw-in.

Question 9   The referee should tell the opponent that he cannot do this, and that he must not impede the thrower.

Question 10   (a) Goal kick; (b) corner kick.

Question 11   The referee should have the throw-in re-taken. It is impossible to play the advantage from a foul throw.

Question 12   The referee should stop the game and send off the culprit for violent conduct. The game must re-start with the goal kick because the ball was not in play at the time since it had not left the penalty area.

Question 13   Re-take the goal kick. Again, the ball has not left the penalty area and is thus not in play.

Question 14   When it goes into the goal direct from: (a) an indirect free kick; (b) a throw-in; (c) a dropped ball; (d) a kick-off.

Question 15   Award an indirect free kick from the place where the player made contact with the ball for a second time. The ball must be touched by a second player before the kicker may play it again, and the post does not count in this respect.

Question 16   Yes.

REFEREES WANTED

Throughout the country local football depends on the services of keen, dedicated people who make a vast contribution to the national game as referees, enabling players to more easily enjoy their matches.

CAN YOU HELP?

Every year more clubs are registered with The Football Association. There are more and more matches to which referees must be appointed.

CAN YOU HELP?

If you have played the game at any level you will know how important it is to have a qualified referee present.

CAN YOU HELP?

If you are physically fit, with good eyesight and are at least fourteen years of age and willing to attend a local course of instruction, in preparation for a straight forward examination,

WILL YOU HELP?

If you are interested in accepting the challenge of refereeing local football matches

PLEASE CONTACT:–

THE FOOTBALL ASSOCIATION
16 LANCASTER GATE,
LONDON W2 3LW.

quoting referee recruitment or your local County Football Association. Don't forget that today's top referees all started at this level.
This is the first rung on the ladder.

Index